LETTERS
— FROM THE —
INSIDE:

Hope in the Journey Beyond
Classroom and Cell

Bronwyn Harris

and

Jorge Ramirez

Copyright © 2020 by Bronwyn Harris

All rights reserved. This book or any portion thereof may not be reproduced or used in any manner whatsoever without the express written permission of the publisher except for the use of brief quotations in a book review.

Editor: *Julia Watson-Foster*
Copyeditors: *Philip Dangler and Christine Osborne*
Author Photograph: *Omar Rodriguez*
Cover Design: *Erinn Larsen*
Book Composition: *Marites D. Bautista*

1 2 3 4 5 6 7 8 9 0
ISBN-13: 979-8655441583
www.bronwynharris.com

For my beloved mother: thank you for being the best mother you could have been and for all that you did for me. Out of everything in this world, I wasn't expecting to lose you, but I know you're in a better place and always by my side looking over me. Until we meet again, I love you, Mom!

For my loving grandmother, thank you for all the support you show me and for the wonderful job you did in raising me. Without your strength and dedication, I wouldn't be the man I am today!

Last but not least, for my beautiful fiancée, thank you for coming into my life and filling my heart with so much love and joy. I know the circumstances of all this aren't the best but I know our love and nothing is going to get in the way of that. Things will only get better and soon we'll be living our happily ever after. I love you, Joanna!

—Jorge Ramirez | Undisclosed Prison in California, 2020

ஐ ✻ ஓ

To Symphony, Thomas, and Lucille: may you always listen to other people's stories and continue to make the world a better place

—Bronwyn Harris | Alameda California, 2020

CONTENTS

- FOREWORD vii
- INTRODUCTION 1
- JORGE'S STORY 3
- HOW THIS BOOK CAME ABOUT 5
- AFTERWORD BY JORGE 161
- ACKNOWLEDGMENTS 167
- AFTERWORD 169

FOREWORD

If you need fuel to encourage educators, you're holding it in your hands. This book illuminates the depth of relationship that can form between teachers and students, even in the worst-case scenario—when the distressing "school-to-prison pipeline" claims yet another at-risk young person.

Reading *Letters from the Inside* is the next best thing to joining us in person when we visit Jorge, Bronwyn's former student and co-author. It's early when we hit the road. After we greet each other, Jorge's Abuela hands out homemade tamales for the three-hour journey. We're stocked up with dollar bills for the food vending machines and have done our best to comply with dress codes to avoid problems through the security checkpoints. Along the way, we chat and laugh, Jorge's sister and fiancée put headphones on or fall asleep, Abuela gazes out at passing farms, perhaps remembering the Salvadoran village of her childhood, Bronwyn knits or naps, and I drive.

Nowadays, visiting Jorge feels almost routine, but the first time we visited a few years ago, Bronwyn was nervous. Would her former student be happy to see her? Would their old connection hold strong more than a decade after it was formed?

We made it through the dehumanizing security checkpoints, walked along barbed wire under armed surveillance, and entered a more welcoming area where families and friends chatted with people "on the inside." I remember the moment when Jorge entered and saw his old teacher; I'll forever associate the metaphor of a "face lighting up" with that encounter. He glowed at the sight of her, and her welcoming smile was just as full of joy.

Since then, the connection between these two—teacher and student—has proven to be deep, dear, and unbreakable. Bronwyn writes, sends packages, keeps an eye on Jorge's family's needs, and visits regularly. I watch in amazement as she jokes, listens, encourages, and helps him set and meet goals—practices that seem to come as naturally as breathing to an excellent educator. In turn, Jorge offers her the respect and responsiveness of a top-notch student.

I invite you to read on and discover the wonder of a teacher-student bond that endured despite the best efforts of an evil system to sever it. Sociological terms like "pipelines" and disheartening statistics about crime and students in urban schools don't have the last word. Love does, thank God, and always will.

— Mitali Perkins | Martinez California, 2020

INTRODUCTION

I was nervous the first time I walked into the prison, which I suppose is normal. I wasn't sure if my old student Jorge would recognize me, and I was worried that he'd hate what I had written about him. I wasn't sure if we'd have anything to talk about, or if I'd feel unsafe. But when you're a teacher who tells your students they'll always be "your kids," no matter what, you may have to visit someone in prison.

In my previous book, *Literally Unbelievable: Stories from an East Oakland Classroom*, I told condensed life stories of some of the kids I taught in my third-grade class over the years. During the process of writing that book, when at all possible, I checked in on those former students, making sure that they were comfortable with what I wrote about them. But when it came to Jorge, whose story is the subject of Chapter Ten in *Literally Unbelievable*, I didn't know how to contact him. So I ran a Google search. What I found broke my heart, but it didn't entirely surprise me. Jorge had been arrested, along with another gang member, shortly after he turned eighteen, for aiding in an attempted shooting of Oakland police officers.

A reporter friend checked into the story for me and found that Jorge was at a well-known California prison, and provided me with a phone number so I could try contacting him. When I called, it turned out I didn't have all the required information needed about him. The bored employee on the line was about to hang up when I said, "Please. He was my third-grade student." There was a long pause and then she offered to look him up for me in a roundabout way, even though she wasn't supposed to. With her help, I got Jorge's prisoner number and wrote him a letter. It took a while, as I wasn't sure what to say. I struggled and finally came to the conclusion that what I wrote was much less important than the fact that I wrote at all.

Jorge was quick to write back, and we began to exchange letters frequently. I started out thinking we might write once in a while, but before long, our correspondence became almost weekly. This was not the only assumption on my part that I had to quickly dismiss. Initially I thought I'd be dispensing advice and care in a one-sided manner, continuing to act as a mentor to Jorge, as I had when he was a boy. On the contrary, the care and concern went both ways. Jorge was eager to learn all about my life these days and keep track of how I was doing. He thanked me for what I'd done for him and his family over the years and offered his prayers and thoughts, as well as future help in whatever I needed.

Our shared history made it possible for us to reconnect in a deeply meaningful way.

JORGE'S STORY

I first met Jorge when he was eight years old. His teacher, Elise, was a friend of mine, and we sometimes met outside school to pray for the safety and care for our students, because these were kids we cared about and, unfortunately, had good reason to worry about. I was teaching third grade, and she told me that she was requesting that a student currently in her second-grade class be placed with me the following year because he needed "someone who would really take care of him."

She went on to tell me about a particularly heartbreaking and introspective question that this boy, Jorge, had posed in class. "Mrs. Williams," he asked her, "How can I learn to be good?" She asked for clarification and he continued, "Well, other kids have parents who can teach them how to be good. I don't. So how can I learn to be good?"

His fears were legitimate. Jorge didn't have parents who could teach him much of anything. His mother loved him deeply but, having become a parent at age fourteen with Jorge, she struggled with alcohol and drugs for her entire adult life and was frequently absent. He worried about her in the way that she should have worried about him. His father was rarely around, surfacing once in a while to see Jorge and his brother Luis, then disappearing again just as quickly. Jorge's grandmother, who he calls "Tita" (from *Abuelita*, a nickname for "grandmother" in Spanish), was his primary caregiver. She was not much older than many of his friends' mothers. And though she loves him and the other grandchildren in her care fiercely, she faced many challenges—having to work multiple jobs to make ends meet, not speaking English, and never having learned to read and write in Spanish or English.

The fall rolled around, and Jorge was placed in my third-grade class. It was evident right away that he was a remarkable child. He was highly intelligent, able to switch in and out of Spanish and English, and often helped me translate for parents when my conversational Spanish failed me. He was responsible, taking care of the adults as well as the other children in his family. Jorge was also quick to anger, feeling keenly the unfairness of his life and the weight of the world he carried on his shoulders. In addition, he was extremely kind; he cared about me and the community of our classroom.

What I remember most about Jorge in those years, however, was his introspection. When Elise related the story of him wanting to learn how to be good, I knew there was a self-awareness that was unusual in eight-year-old children, and this characteristic was obvious through the year I had him in my classroom. Sometimes he was funny in how he expressed this. Even though he knew how to do it, he rarely turned in his homework. Poking fun at himself, he once made me a flyer that proclaimed, in large letters, "The News for the Day: Jorge Did His Homework!" Other times he broke my heart with his realizations. "Ms. Harris," he said to me once. "I figured something out! When your mom uses drugs, it's not that she doesn't love you anymore, it's that she forgets she loves you." His reflection was the kind of statement that an empathetic teacher could never forget.

All teachers have students that they keep in touch with after the school year ends, and Jorge and his brother Luis were those students for me. As I described in *Literally Unbelievable*, we did a lot together, and I got to know them well. We became more like family friends or an auntie and nephews than a teacher and former students. I went to family events with the brothers, took them to museums and beaches, and helped their mother with school meetings and apartment-hunting. Tragedy struck when one of Jorge's good friends lost his life to gang violence, gunned down right in front of Jorge. They were both thirteen at the time. The lasting trauma that Jorge experienced from this fateful event caused him to act out in ways that, while understandable, were extremely destructive. As he grew more and more angry with his life circumstances, we began to lose touch, and eventually he changed his phone number. I didn't hear from him again until he answered my letter from prison.

HOW THIS BOOK CAME ABOUT

I began my teaching career in East Oakland in January 2000, teaching first-graders who had already gone through one teacher and six substitutes during that school year. In my first five minutes in front of that class, a student threw a book at my head and I realized I had no set curriculum with which to teach them. What's more, I was a "roving teacher," meaning that I moved classrooms every three weeks. It was a challenging introduction to my profession.

As I transitioned into teaching third grade, things didn't get much easier, but my students were incredible. Creative, thoughtful, and loving, they were also angry, misunderstood, at-risk, and largely overlooked by the system. Like many young teachers, I came into the classroom as an idealist, thinking I was going to change the world one student at a time. While I continue to hope I made an impact, I quickly learned that the community was rich in both diversity and care for their children, and largely made up of a network of caring parents, guardians, and extended family, all struggling to bring up healthy, well-adjusted children in the face of the poverty and violence that characterized their neighborhood. I grew to love my students and their families, and was honored to be accepted as part of this village involved in raising their children.

But this also took its toll on my health, and after eight years, I had to face the fact this kind of work was no longer sustainable for me—not under the conditions we faced. In my time at this school, we had a different principal every single year, taught during lockdowns (well before they became "standard procedure" at even the best suburban schools), and never had sufficient supplies. In addition, high-stakes testing put ever-mounting pressure on the faculty. Forcing myself to go on, day in and day out, was making me sick, tired, and miserable. So I left the school, going on to work as Director of Education at Harbor House Ministries in Oakland and then as a private tutor, while volunteering with Big Brothers Big Sisters and working alongside Children Rising.

Over the years, I kept a blog about my experiences as a teacher, and there were countless times that someone read the blog and responded, or I found myself discussing something that had happened in my classroom, and was met with utter disbelief—particularly by middle-class white friends and acquaintances. They simply couldn't fathom the inequities and stark realities that characterized my students' lives—or that such things were possible in current-day America.

I wrote my first book because those conversations showed me there was a need for my kids' stories to be told on a wider scale, and for people to understand the impact that poverty, institutionalized racism, and bad policy decisions have on the lives of real children. Since then, *Literally Unbelievable* has seen considerable success as an Amazon bestseller in its genre. Renowned author and social justice activist Anne Lamott called it "lovely, important, heartbreaking, inspiring…" Concerned Californians have bought dozens of books to send to legislators and other policymakers in order to make them aware of the realities of educational inequality. Since that book came out, I've traveled around the state of California speaking on the topic of education and justice for *all* of our nation's children. I've spoken across the state—in San Diego, Sonoma County, Sacramento and points in-between—Rotary Clubs, churches, book clubs, and teacher preparation programs. I've recently had the privilege of meeting with the California State Assembly's Education Committee. In a wonderful coincidence, I learned that one of the committee staffers taught at the same school I did, having left just a couple of years before I began work there.

After my first letter to Jorge, we began writing on a regular basis. I learned more about what his life had been like after we lost touch, and he asked me what I had been doing since I had left the classroom. With each letter, I felt less like I was talking to a student and more like I was talking to a friend. I learned about a new tragedy in his life: his mother died in a fire and he was unable to go to her memorial service, which added to his sorrow and depression. I told him that I was writing a book about my time teaching, and nervously awaited his response. He was extremely supportive. I told him that I was being honest about what had happened in his life, and again anxiously waited for his answer. Fortunately, when I saw him in person for the first time in almost a decade, he hugged me and told me that he really loved the book—everything about it. He mentioned that he had no idea that anyone was unaware of how hard life was for kids like him. That's when we started discussing the possibility of writing a book together.

We decided that the letters we had been writing told the full story. Our letters explored our reconnection and the reality of his life "on the inside." This book begins with the first letter I wrote, back when I found out where he was and was hoping that I was writing to the correct Jorge. It includes nearly three years of correspondence, up until he finally began studying for the GED and has become more hopeful about his future.

In our society, convicts are either forgotten or vilified. Yes, they've made bad decisions. But behind each prisoner is a story of how they got there. This is Jorge's story, but it's also my story. Having known him when he was young, I watched him get sucked into the school-to-prison pipeline and was powerless to stop it. He definitely made destructive choices, but he was also set up for failure: the adults in his life were uneducated and didn't know their rights, and authority figures abused their power. He went to a profoundly underfunded and subpar school. And he had zero community support whatsoever. The school-to-prison pipeline is not just an abstract concept, but a real institutional structure that ruins real lives.

In writing these letters, I became reacquainted with Jorge. I learned about him, not just as a child and a student, but as a person forced to mature far too quickly in order to take care of himself and his family. I saw the difficult and dangerous decisions he had to make, paradoxically, to keep himself safe. I think differently now about people who are incarcerated. The stories behind each path to prison is as varied as the people facing these sentences. Each almost certainly involved bad decisions, but all too many also stemmed from lack of opportunities, pain, trauma, neglect, and more.

My hope is that any reader of this this book remembers and understands that all inmates were once children. They are still sons and daughters, grandkids, and people's babies. This one story is typical of so many more: we should all understand that trauma leads to actions that may cause someone to become incarcerated and can come to this realization without condoning their actions. It's often easier to see the world in black and white, good and bad, but we must understand that people are complicated and that the inequity in opportunities, institutional privilege, and outright racism all play a role in who commits crimes and who is jailed.

June 23, 2016

Dear Jorge,

First of all, do you still go by Jorge? And you are my former student, right? I can't imagine there's another person with your exact name, but you never know. If you're the right Jorge, tell me your brother's name!

I've been thinking about you and Googled you; that's how I found you. I've been thinking about you and praying for you a lot. In fact, I just found a letter you wrote me—or more like a sign or announcement. It says, "The news from Jorge! I did my homework!" I've kept it for twelve or thirteen years now.

I am writing a book about teaching in Oakland, so I've been thinking about my students quite a lot. You all had it rough. I mean, life is really unfair. I wish I could have done more for all of you.

That said, you've got to make your own decisions. Seems like you've made some bad ones, and I really hope that changes. I don't know what you can do to make your life better there, but I hope you do.

I will keep praying. If you want to write to me, I'll write back. If I got the right Jorge!

—Ms. Harris

July 6, 2016

Hey Ms. Harris,

I'm happy to hear from you. It's been a long time. Yeah, I still go by Jorge and I am your former student. I'm the only one with this name. That's crazy how you found me on Google. I've been thinking a lot about you too. I can't believe you still have that sign I made. You've had that for a long time. That's nice that you're writing a book about teaching in Oakland. I'll have to read it once it's done.

But life is unfair. It seems like right after we lost contact, I started making bad decisions. I joined a gang, started using guns for what reason, I don't know. But I regret everything. I'm not a gang member anymore. I dropped out[1] cause I'm trying to change my life and better myself, you know. I took nineteen years with a strike, that was the last offer they gave me. It was either that or go to trial and get eighty-four to life, so I had no choice but to take the nineteen years. I really regret doing what I did but I can't do nothing about it now, just try and better myself, get in all the programs they got to offer, get my GED, and find a trade.

The good thing is they have this youth offender program for people under the age of twenty-three and they help you get out early. And out of the nineteen years I'm only doing sixteen years.

And with the youth offender program I might get out even earlier. I'm just happy none of my brothers chose my path, you know. The sad thing is my mom just passed away on December 28, last year, in a house fire. That really messed me up, but she's up there with God now in a better place. It was really nice to hear from you, and it would be nice to see you again. I'm going to send you a visiting form. If you ever want to visit me just fill it out and send it back to me. I'll be waiting on your letter.

Love,
Jorge

---

[1] Left the gang.

July 9, 2016

Dear Jorge,

I was so glad to hear from you and relieved that I wrote to the right person. You just had a birthday, right? How old are you now?

I am so sorry to hear about your mom. Who is taking care of the kids? What is Luis doing now? Does your family visit you?

Life is very unfair. And it's been particularly unfair to you. I'm not excusing your bad decisions, I think you know that, but I think you've been treated very badly by life and other people, and I can understand the anger that probably led to a lot of your bad decisions.

I really hope and pray that you are able to change your life. But tell me the truth, OK? Not just what you think I want to hear.

So tell me what programs you're in there? Can you get your GED? Do you need any books for that?

Also, do you have a Bible? And if so, is it one that is easy to read or no? I'd be happy to send you any of these.

I have a whole chapter in my book about you and Luis and Joshua. I am still so sad about that, and I don't know if you're more sad or angry, but it was horrible. I also wrote about our Exploratorium trip—do you remember how fun that was? I've changed your names in the book.

I'll think about visiting. I'd like to see you, but it would be hard for me as well. I will definitely keep writing if you want, and if you want any books, let me know.

—Ms. Harris

(And I do believe you can make your life better, I really do)

July 15, 2016

Dear Jorge,

I hope this book gets to you. It looks like it's OK to send books, but of course I don't know all the rules. I read this book [*Tattoos on the Heart*] a while ago, and it has a lot of people who get second chances! I hope you get a second chance from yourself, if that makes any sense. It's going to take hard work, but you can do it.

Are there any other books you want or need?

I have the visitor form. Do I mail it back to you or somewhere else?

Has anyone visited you?

I'll write more later.

Love,
Ms. Harris

July 20, 2016

Hey Ms. Harris,

I'm happy that you found me too. Yes, I just had a birthday. I turned 21 years old. I know it's messed up what happened to my mom but you know what they say things happened for a reason. I just know she's in a better place now. I don't know if you remember my mom's husband. He has Clarissa, Ali, and Junior. Do you remember my other brother and sister Karla and Angel? Well my grandma just got custody of Karla and Angel is still with his dad. My grandma was vising me in the county jail but since I been here I haven't got no visits.

Life is unfair and I'm not excusing my bad decisions either. I also don't blame nobody for what I did, but due to the fact that I got treated badly by other people and life is what led me to acting the way I did.

I am going to change my life and that's the truth. I want to become a better person and not just for me but for my family also. Because I got family that needs me to be out there. I also need to be out there for all my brothers and sisters, and it hurts that I can't be out there for them now when they need me the most, but I'll be there for them when I get out.

Right now where I'm at it's just a reception center. I'm only here until I get endorsed into another prison. But once I get to a mainline, I'm going to go to school so I can get my GED. Then I'm going to learn a trade. I'd appreciate it if you could send me some studying material so I can be prepared for it. I really want to get my high school diploma so if there's any programs for that, that's what I'm going to do.

Also I do have a Bible but the one I have is hard for me to understand. I'll be happy if you can send me one I can understand better.

I would like to read your book when you're done with it. It's pretty cool to know I'm going to be in a book. I'm sad and angry about what happened to

Joshua[2] but he's in a better place now. And I do remember the Exploratorium trip, it was lots of fun.

Well, if you decide to visit, just fill out the visiting form and send it back to me. And I appreciate you writing me. You and my brother are the only people who write me. If you send me books, I like conspiracy books, cultural books, really any type of books as long as it's good. Also, I don't want to be asking for too much but you can also send me writing packages like books of stamps, pens but they have to be clear (like see-through), writing paper, and envelopes. You don't have to send me that but if you decide to I would highly appreciate it.

Do you remember my girlfriend? Well I'm not with her no more. Before I came here I was in the county jail for two years and a year after I was there she just stopped talking to me and I haven't heard from her since. She's one of the reasons why I been stressing, you know because I was with her for so long so it's kinda hard for me not being with her. But I'll be all right. Luis just turned 18. He's going to school. He's been good for the most part.

I have a question, do you still have pictures of the times you took us out, like to the Exploratorium? If you do, do you think you can send me some please?

Well, I'll talk to you soon.

Love,
Jorge

---

[2] Jorge's friend Joshua was murdered in front of him when they were both 13.

July 20, 2016

Dear Ms. Harris,

Hey, I got that book that you sent me. It seems like a good book. Thank you too I really needed it 'cause I have no books to read. Whenever you talk to Mrs. Williams or Mr. Jackson tell them I said hi. Also Ms. Gibson. Now with the visiting form you send that back to me when you write me a letter. Then it takes like two to four weeks for you to clear but after like two weeks you should start calling up here to the prison to check if you cleared then when you clear you can make a visit. The visits up here are like an hour and a half long. I haven't got no visit from nobody yet. Hopefully I'll get one soon.

Love,
Jorge

July 26, 2016

Dear Jorge,

Well, I think you probably got my visitor form. I'm hoping to come Thursday, August 25 if everything is processed and it's OK with you. I thought visiting hours would be just weekends, but the website said Thursdays, too. Is that right?

Your handwriting is so much better than mine! Maybe I should type letters. I sent you one GED prep book, so let me know if you got it. I also asked some of my friends if they'd send books, so if you hear from random people, that's why. I hope you like the books! And you can write back to them or not, of course, your choice.

So if it is just a reception center, do you know when or to where or when you'll be moved? Just write me if you get moved so I know.

Do you want to tell me about what life is like in prison/jail or no? I don't know if it's helpful to talk about it.

If you're in touch with Luis, please tell him I'd love to hear from him. You have my address, but he can also call or text. Is he with your grandma?

I will look for photos. It might take a few weeks because I have to get them printed from the computer. I think I have Waterworld photos. Remember that trip?

So, books. I think I sent you an easier Bible. I love things like *Harry Potter* even though they are supposedly kids' books because they're so good and you can escape into them. Is that OK or no young adult books? What else? *The Hunger Games* is good. I'll keep thinking but tell me if you have requests. Reading is a very good way to make your life better. Reading, writing, and praying.

Speaking of praying, is there any kind of Bible Study or prison fellowship? Try to surround yourself with positive people as much as you can. You might not have much choice, but you have to do the best with what you have.

The chapter about you and Luis was hard to write; I'm not going to lie. I can tell you the basic outline of it if you want. It was so hard to see you both go through so much pain and try so hard to take care of your mom even when she was making bad decisions.

The article I read said you shot at a police officer. Was he hurt?

I am praying for you.

Love,
Ms. Harris

July 30, 2016

Hi Ms. Harris,

I got the visiting form. They usually take out the form and just give me the envelope with a stamp saying they removed the visiting form. Now that the form is here, they're going to check your background. Once you clear I'll get a notice saying you cleared, but if you don't clear they won't notify me, but you'll get something in the mail saying why you didn't get approved. Once you get approved I'll let you know then you will have to call up here and make a visit. They say they have you on hold for a while but don't hang up. Visiting days are Thursday, Saturday, Sunday, and holidays from eight to one-thirty and visits are one hour long. I'm also endorsed to another prison already. I don't know exactly where it's at but I heard it's close by to Sacramento.

I'm also a level three. I got fifty-eight points. I don't know if you know but in prison it goes from level one all the way to level four and it goes by points. I don't know what's the points for a level one or two but all I know is I'm two points away form a level four. Sixty points and up is a level four. That's why I'm staying out of trouble because I'm not trying to go to a level four. I'll write more later. Take care.

Love,
Jorge

August 4, 2016

Dear Ms. Harris,

Yeah, I got that visiting form. It usually takes anywhere from two to five weeks for you to clear, but once you clear I'll get a notice saying you cleared then it's up to me to let you know. So I'll let you know once you clear. Yep, there's visiting on Thursday, Saturday, and Sundays.

You really think my handwriting is good? I thought my writing was ugly. I wish I could type letters. That would be fun but then again, writing gives me something to do. I haven't got that GED prep book yet but I'll probably get it sometime this week. I'll let you know when I get it. It's all right and speaking of that I got a letter from one of your friends somebody named Emily, I'm going to write her back.

Well, when you first get here you have to wait until you see your counselor then when you see him, he talks to you about how many points you have and what two prisons you would like to go to. After you give him your two options then a few weeks after that you have to put in a form to see if you're endorsed and what prison you're endorsed to.

Well the county jail was all right but prison is real crazy and dangerous. There's always fights and every time somebody fights, COs start spraying pepper spray. Then they have a gunner and if the people that are fighting don't get down right away the gunner starts shooting with a block gun.[3] And if you're around the people that are fighting, you better be careful because they don't care who they hit.

The second day I was here at dinner at the table I was sitting at they jumped somebody. The COs started spraying pepper spray and I almost got hit with the block gun. That was crazy. The cells are real small. You can barely move

---

[3] A block gun (also called a riot gun or non-lethal launcher) is a firearm often used in prisons to control inmates. They fire ammunition such as bean bag rounds or rubber bullets to suppress riots.

around. You're locked up in your cell all day, You can only go out for breakfast and dinner to the dining hall. They give us yard twice a week for two hours on Wednesdays and Saturdays, but it's a small yard. One thing I hate the most is the showers because there's like thirty-five men in there at the same time. There's eight shower heads and we only get fifteen minutes to shower. I hate that.

Whenever Luis writes me I'll give him your number so he can contact you, and yes he is still living with my grandma. I also still do remember Waterworld, that was fun.

I haven't got that Bible you sent. Maybe sometime this week. I never read the *Harry Potter* books but I think I can get into it. *The Hunger Games* I read all of those when I was in the county jail. They were good, I like them.

They don't have Bible studies here in reception. Maybe when I get to another prison they will.

And about your book I'd rather just read the book when you're done writing it. I'm also happy that you guys agree that I'm a good person because I am a good person. I just made some bad decisions, and now that I'm in here it's just time for me to focus on myself and become a better person.

The officer did not get hurt. Nobody got hurt. Only the car got hit.

Thank you for the extra paper and envelopes I really appreciate it. And the books, try sending them through Amazon so they can have my name and they won't take it away because it doesn't have my name.

But anyway, hope to hear from you soon.

Love,
Jorge

August 11, 2016

Dear Jorge,

OK, let me know if you get any of the books. Amazon says they're delivered but I have no idea how long it takes to actually get to you once they are at the prison. I hope you get them!

Visiting on Thursday, August 25 will work for me if they clear my paperwork by then. If not, it'll be September.

Emily told me she'd write. She's in my writing group and was telling us she misses writing letters. I thought you might like more mail.

I didn't know about the points system. Is there a way to get points taken off or just added? I'm glad you're trying to stay out of trouble. It seems like the more you can study, read, and write, those are probably the best ways to spend your time. Can you exercise at all?

It does sound crazy and dangerous. I wish prisons did more to actually change people's lives for the better rather than just punishing people.

I have always thought your handwriting was good!

I'll send photo and paper and envelopes next time. Here's a bookmark for my book. When it comes out, on Oct 1, I'll send you a copy. I don't know if they'll let me send you a signed copy, or if I'll have to send it straight from Amazon.

Do you ever keep a journal? Writing things down might help you process things. I can only imagine how much anger must build up.

I'll send you *Harry Potter*. Tell me if you like the first one because there are seven. I love it even though it's for kids; it's a really good series.

Yes, when you get to the new prison, look for Bible Studies. It will be good, positive energy for you. There are people praying for you.

I'm glad the officer wasn't hurt, and yes, I think you are a good person. Good people can make bad decisions. We all make bad decisions, of course, just at different levels of impact. And you weren't given many examples of how to be emotionally healthy. But I believe you can change that now.

Let me know if you get the books.

Love,
Ms. Harris

August 21, 2016

Dear Jorge,

Well, I haven't gotten any word about visiting, and I tried to call but can't get anywhere with that, so I don't think they'll let me come on Thursday. I'll try to find another day and hopefully hear from them soon. Do you know when you will be transferred?

By the way, if you want to write to any elected officials explaining your situation/story, I am happy to help you find names and addresses. There is some prison reform going on, and I think hearing from prisoners would be good.

How are you doing in terms of discouragement/anger/boredom? What helps you? Writing? Praying? Reading? Sleeping? I'm praying for you a lot, and I keep sending people to write to you but of course you don't ever have to answer if you don't want to.

My dog is getting surgery tomorrow. She tore her ACL, which is a ligament in her knee, although I think it's called something else in dogs. It's an injury that a lot of human athletes get. She'll be fine and she gets to exercise just as much when it heals, but it's really expensive. And it's always hard to take a dog into surgery because they don't know why they're hurting. I had my tonsils out in March, and that was super painful but at least I knew why and that it was going to get better.

My friend Emily said she was impressed with both your handwriting and your writing. See, I told you your handwriting was great!

My book is coming out on October 1st! I am excited and also pretty scared. I have to do events and try to market it myself because I'm self-publishing. But I think sharing all your stories is so important. People need to know what it was like for you all. So I changed your name, but I told your whole story—the good and the bad (we all have both). I hope you will feel respected.

Have you gotten any more books? Do you need a journal or anything?

Love,
Ms. Harris

August 21, 2016

Hi Ms. Harris,

I haven't got those books yet but if it said it's delivered then I should be getting them soon. Hopefully you're cleared by that date. If not I'll see you in September. I'll get a notice once you're cleared, so I'll let you know when I get it.

Yeah, I actually got a letter from her the same day I got your letter. It's pretty cool to have somebody else to write. You know the only people I write is Luis, you, and now Emily. So it's nice to have somebody else to talk to. I don't know when I'll be going there. All I know is I'm waiting on a bus to pick me up and take me there.

What do you mean by wanting to change now? Do you mean change as in changing my life and becoming a better person? If that's what you mean then yes, I do want to change. I just need to get out of this reception center because being locked up in this cell all day is driving me crazy.

Yeah, you can get points added and taken off. You get points added by fighting or doing other stuff you're not supposed to, every writeup adds six points. And if you do good and don't get in trouble for a whole year, they take off twelve points every year for good time. That's all I do is read, write letters, and exercise every other day.

I'm glad you started writing me. I get happy when I get a letter in the mail. And mail means a lot in this place. That's why I said it's cool that you had Emily write me because I don't get mail except from my brother and now you guys.

I got your bookmark. I like your picture; is that picture recent? I think it would be better to just send the book through Amazon so the book can have my name and CDC # on it.

I don't have a journal, but it would be a good idea to write things down when I'm mad or when I just want to express myself. I got the article, it was easy to read. Thank you for sending it.

Once I get the *Harry Potter* book I'll let you know if I like it. I heard it was a really good series, so I'll probably like it. When I get to where I'm going I'm getting into all the programs they have to offer to keep me occupied. Now that I'm in here it's now time for me to become a better person for myself and my family.

I'll let you know when I get those books. Hope to hear from you soon.

Take care.

Love,
Jorge

August 24, 2016

Hi Ms. Harris,

I got those pictures today. It's nice looking at them and they bring back memories. By the way, thank you for sending them. I'll let you know as soon as I get any book.

It's all right if your friends want to write me. I'll write back, but as long as you keep writing me back that's all I care about, you know :)

And about your friend wanting to send me food, well here in reception you can't send food packages, you can only send writing packages. Once I get to where I'm supposed to go, then you can send me food, clothes, and stuff like that. When I get to where I'm going I'll write you and explain exactly how it works if they still want to do it.

I also just wanted to tell you that I got a lot of love for you Ms. Harris and I'm thankful and really appreciate you. Ever since me and my brother were kids, you were always a positive influence in my life. You know you always took us out to a lot of different places and if it wasn't for you I would have never experienced none of those places. And in this place where I'm at like there's people that don't have nobody at all to write them so I'm grateful that I have people like you to write. It shows a lot.

So I just wanted to tell you that I'm thankful to have you in my life, Ms. Harris. Thank you for the pictures and I hope to hear from you soon.

Talk to you soon.

Love,
Jorge

August 28, 2016

Hi Ms. Harris,

I'm just writing you this quick letter letting you know that I got transferred to the new prison on Friday the 26th. I don't know if you wrote me at the old one, but if you did it's going to take a little longer for me to get the mail, but I'll get it. So you can let Emily know that I'm over here now so she won't be writing the old prison no more.

Right now I'm on orientation which means I can't go out the cell for a week until I go see committee. After I see committee I'll be able to get out of the cell. I'll be able to use the phone. I'll be programming like everybody else. After I get cleared, I'll be able to get contact visits so I'm looking forward to that. Anyway, I just wanted to let you know I'm over here now so write me over here. Hope to hear from you soon. Take care.

Love,
Jorge

September 1, 2016

Dear Jorge,

Thank you for letting me know you got transferred. I tried sending books again so just let me know if it works.

I'm really glad I found you too. You know how much I care about all my students, including you and Luis, and I remember saying that you'd always be "my kids."

So what are the main differences between the two prisons? Did you get a work assignment? Do they have yoga? I feel like you might make fun of yoga at first, but it can be really calming and feel great.

I found a few photos of my current dog, Ruby. She's not Solomon, but she's pretty awesome.

OK, I have to go to work but wanted to make sure you know I got your letter about moving. Let me know if you get any books. The only one you've gotten is *Tattoos on the Heart*, right?

Love,
Ms. Harris

September 6, 2016

Hi Ms. Harris,

Today my counselor came to see me and, well, the good news is he said I'm getting off orientation on Wednesday which is tomorrow. Now the bad news is he's talking about I have an ICE hold[4] and that I'm an immigrant. He says that it shows I was born in Mexico. I told him I don't know what he's talking about. I told him I was born in Oakland and the name of the hospital. He asked me if I had my birth certificate. I told him I can have somebody send it in and he said all right. So I'm going to have Luis send it in. I honestly don't know what that counselor is talking about. I was born here. They must have my name mixed up with somebody else. I just don't want them to confuse me with another person and send me to Mexico for no reason.

Tomorrow I get off orientation but I won't be able to use the phone until Thursday, so I'm going to call her and tell her to have Luis send my birth certificate to me so I can send it to that counselor. I'm kind of mad right now so I felt like I had to talk to somebody. That's why I wrote you this letter letting you know what happened today. Hopefully this situation gets cleared up because that's all I'm thinking about. I don't want to be stressing for nothing when I know I was born here. But anyway talk to you later, I'll let you know what goes on. Take care.

Love,
Jorge

P.S. I wrote this letter before I got your other letter.

---

[4] According to Lena Graber of the National Immigration Project of the National Lawyers Guild (https://www.nilc.org/) "An ICE hold is a request to a jail regarding someone in custody. The request asks the jail to notify ICE when the person will be released, and to hold the person for an extra 48 hours so that ICE has an opportunity to come get them."

September 6, 2016

Hey Ms. Harris,

This place is way better than the other prison. Over here you're not locked up in your cell all day, only during the time you're on orientation. Once you get off you can move around freely. But you either have to work or go to school and you can only have a job if you have a high school diploma or GED and since I don't have none of those two I'm going to have to go to school.

I'm not sure if they have Bible studies yet but I'm pretty sure they do. I'm going to have to look into it.

Ruby looks cool. Have you taken her to the snow?

I'll let you know if I get any books. The only one I've gotten so far is *Tattoos On the Heart*. By the way, I read it already. It was a good book.

Talk to you later.

Love,
Jorge

September 7, 2016

Dear Jorge,

How is the new prison? Has your schedule been set yet?

I tried sending you some books at the new place, so let me know if you get any of them.

It's very hot today so no one wants to do anything. I bet it's even hotter where you are. It's supposed to cool down tomorrow though. Then pretty soon it will get cold, and I hate the cold. I'm such a weather wimp!

My dog just had knee surgery. She was in a lot of pain the first couple of days and then she felt better, and now I just have to stop her from exercising, which is really hard! She's quite an athlete!

What kind of programs do they have at the new prison?

I'm working a lot right now—tutoring kids, writing, and working on my book, which is coming out on October 1st! I'm kind of scared about it coming out. It will be very public and not everyone will be happy with what I say.

Well, let me know how you are doing!

Love,
Ms. Harris

September 11, 2016

Hi Jorge,

I'm glad you wrote when you were feeling angry and frustrated. You can always talk (write) to me. I hope it helps a little to get your feelings out that way. And I agree, it's totally unfair that they need your birth certificate! You're an American citizen! You were born in Oakland, right? I hope it can get sorted out ASAP.

If your grandma doesn't have the birth certificate, you can get it from the hospital. I've had to order copies of mine before. It depends on the hospital if you have to pay, but it's not much if you do.

Yes, please send a couple of visitor forms. I don't know when I can make it up there, but I will at some point. I have a friend who is willing to drive with me and can come in for a few minutes if you want more visitors. And if your brother ever needs a ride to visit, tell him to contact me and we'll figure something out. I don't know what days are visiting days or when I can get there, but it'll happen.

My book is out on October 1st, so that's part of why I don't know my schedule. I have one book reading on October 1st to celebrate the release and one in San Diego on October 9th, and I don't know yet if there will be more. I hope so. I think all of your stories deserve to be told.

I'm nervous for you and my other former students to read it though, because I'm very honest. I don't use your real names, but I talk about bad choices you made as well as how wonderful you were and also how hard it was for you all in Oakland and how the schools/police treated you. So I'm not sure if you'll be totally happy with me telling all the truth. But again, I didn't use your name, and I tried to do it very respectfully. You can tell me if I succeeded.

Did you get any of the books from Amazon? Let me know. I'll mail this now and write in more detail soon. I hope you're doing well, and please keep me updated on the programs you're in, etc. I'm glad you liked *Tattoos on the Heart*. I want to visit their bakery where they employ former gang members next time I'm in LA. I really appreciated that book and their work.

Love,
Ms. Harris

September 17, 2016

Hi Ms. Harris,

This new place is all right and it's way better now that I'm off orientation. I haven't been assigned to anything yet, so I'm still waiting. My schedule is the same every day. I wake up at 5:30 AM then we go to breakfast at 6:30 AM. After walk back to the cell and wait for yard release which is at 8:00 AM and you can be outside all day if you want. I always come back in at 11:45 AM because it is too hot out there.

Anyway, I did get three books that you sent. I got the GED prep book, the New Testament Bible, and the Harry Potter book. Then I got a paper for a book you tried sending. It said something about it has to be sent from an approved vendor, but it didn't say which book.

It is very hot here and I hate the heat. I can't wait until the cold comes. Poor doggy, I bet she went through a lot of pain. I hope she gets better soon. I'm not sure which programs they have yet but I know they have GED classes and I think they have college courses also but I don't know what else they have.

Where are you tutoring kids? I would be scared if I was coming out with a book also but I think you'll be fine don't worry.

I am an American citizen. I was born in Oakland. I already told my grandma to send me a copy of my birth certificate so I can clear that up, so I'll be all right.

With the packages it works like this, you can only get four packages a year and they go by weight; the most is 464 oz. And there's a few vendors you can order from. There's Union Supply, Access, Walkenhorst's, and Golden State. Those are some of the vendors they have. Now either she can just order whatever she thinks I like or I can make her a list but she would have to tell me how much she's going to spend. But right now my grandma ordered me some clothes and a pair of shoes so she would have to wait until the next quarter. These are how the quarters work: Quarter 1 Jan 1-Mar 31, Quarter 2 April 1-June 30,

Quarter 3 July 1-Sept 30, Quarter 4 Oct 1-Dec 31. If you want I can let you know when she's able to order me a package.

I'll send you a couple of visiting forms and your friend can come if she likes, no problem. My brother hasn't been approved yet to come visit. Hopefully soon though. My grandma is the only one approved so far. Visiting days are Saturdays and Sundays and you don't have to make an appointment for visits here. You just show up early and they let you in.

I think your book is going to be good and I don't have a problem with you telling the truth. I can't wait to read it. It's kind of cool to know I'm going to be part of a book. I'll let you know what I think of it when I read it.

Here go the visiting forms. Just fill them out and send them back to me. Talk to you soon. Take care.

Love,
Jorge

September 21, 2016

Dear Jorge,

Here's the form back! I'll send one to my friend who might want to come with me too. Her name is Mitali Perkins so if you get a random form or letter from her, you'll know.

So, you told me the beginning of your day's schedule. What's the rest of the day like? You get up really early, so do you go to bed early?

I'm glad you got those three books. Those are a good start. The Bible should be way easier to read than the other one. *Harry Potter* is a great book, and if you like it there are six more in the series. And I really want you to pass the GED! I hope they have classes for it; the book should help. On October 1st, I'll be able to send you a copy of my book from Amazon!

Sorry it's so hot there. That must make everyone irritable. It should cool down soon though.

I mostly tutor kids at my house, but sometimes at theirs or at the library. I had one kid whose teacher was being really rude to him and calling him aggressive and defiant even though he wasn't. So I went with his mom to talk to the principal. The kid is Black and the teacher is white, and I think she doesn't realize she has stereotypes about Black kids. But white kids don't usually get called aggressive and defiant. I wish we had more teachers who were Black and Latino because we really need more perspectives. Did you know that about 82% of all teachers in the United States are white?

What time would we come visit? Do they ever let people come on weekdays or just weekends? Are you allowed to wear your own clothes there, or do you have to wear a uniform?

Ruby the dog is doing much better, thank you. It's hard to see an animal in pain, especially when she's usually such a happy dog.

I'll talk to you soon.

Love,
Ms. Harris

September 26, 2016

Hi Ms. Harris,

I'm doing good. I just got a job in the kitchen and it's all right. I work from 6:00 AM to 8:00 AM, then at 4:00 PM to 6:00 PM, I'm either serving the food or washing the dishes. And yes it's real hot here and I hate the heat but it's cool in the building. You can have fans in your cell too.

With the packages, there's a few vendors you can order from. The ones I know are Walkenhorst's, Access SecurePak, Golden State, and Union Supply. But you can only get one package per quarter and there's four quarters in a year. My grandma just ordered me a package for the fourth quarter so if you would like to order me a package you would have to wait until the beginning of next year. Or you can order a package in my celly's name and I'll still get it. That's if you want to order me a package for this quarter but I don't know if you would like to do it like that. So if you don't you would have to wait until next year so you would have to let me know what you think.

Oh and I got those books that you sent me. The *Harry Potter* book, GED prep book, and the New Testament Bible. I like the *Harry Potter* book and the Bible is real easy to understand. Thank you, Ms. Harris, I really appreciate you.

I also got some books Emily sent me too. I got a visit from my grandma and little sister last week. It was cool, contact visit. I got to hug both of them, I had a really good time.

Also when you write me back put my new bunk number because I'm not in that other building no more.

Anyway, nice hearing from you, talk to you soon.

Love,
Jorge

September 29, 2016

Hi Ms. Harris,

So that form you sent back did you fill it out for you or somebody else? And I'll keep an eye out for your friend. I don't know if I told you yet but I just got a job in the kitchen. I work from 6:00 AM to 8:00 AM then again at 4:00 PM to 6:00 PM. They either have me cleaning the dishes or serving food. It's all right. My days off are Tuesdays and Wednesdays.

I'm also going to sign up for an education program called VEP [Voluntary Education Program] so I can get ready for my GED. I can't wait to read your book!

Yeah, it's really hot over here. That's the only thing I don't like about this prison instead, but that's why I don't stay outside for too long either. It's cooler in the building.

That's messed up that the teacher was calling him names like that and I think you're right. We should have more teachers of different races so things like that don't happen. And I didn't know 82% of teachers in the U.S. are white.

I'm positive you don't need an appointment because my grandma and sister just came to see me about a week ago with no appointment. Visits are from 9:00 in the morning to 2:00 in the afternoon and you can stay for however long you like. Also visits are only Saturday and Sunday. My grandma just ordered me a package. It was supposed to be for the third quarter and it turned out to be for the fourth quarter so I won't be able to get a package until next year. Your friend can order me a package in my celly's name and I'll still get it but I don't know if she would like to do it like that. It would be up to her. Let me know what she thinks.

Yeah, you can wear your own clothes and shoes but you have to wear your state clothes when you're working, going to school, or having visits. I'm waiting on some clothes right now. I'm happy Ruby is doing better.

Oh and did you send me a book called *Long Walk to Freedom* by Nelson Mandela? Because I just got it about two days ago. If it wasn't you most likely it was Emily.

Anyway, nice hearing from you, and talk to you soon.

Love,
Jorge

October 16, 2016

Dear Jorge,

Thanks for the letter! I sent you my book and I hope you like it, but I'm nervous, of course! I think it's really important for people to know what you and other kids went through at our school and in Oakland in general, but I want to make sure you feel respected.

I think I sent you my visiting form. If you didn't get it, something went wrong so please send me another. I do want to visit!

What else is going on? It's pouring rain here. I know we need it, but I don't like going out in the rain. I'm a wimp!

I've been traveling to try to talk to people about my book. I did the book launch party where someone interviewed me and everything (It was very fancy; I felt a little bit like an imposter!) in Alameda. Then I went to San Diego and did another book talk. Next is Sacramento. It's a good thing I'm not that nervous about talking in front of people.

So how many of the books have you had time to read, and which were your favorites? That will help me choose books in the future. And you're taking GED classes now?

I will talk to you soon!

Love,
Ms. Harris

October 27, 2016

Hi Ms. Harris,

I got the books you sent me including the one you wrote. I haven't started reading it yet and I barely got done reading *Harry Potter*. I'm going to read yours next and you don't have to be nervous. I'm pretty sure you did a good job.

Also you and your friend got approved for visiting already, I just got the notice last week. But I just wanted to let you know right, when I was still active in the county jail, there was a riot with the Blacks and the Northerners and I ended up getting jumped by five Black prisoners and I got my front tooth broke. I just wanted to let you know because I really don't like talking about it. I feel embarrassed because I'm only twenty-one and I'm missing a front tooth. They're going to fix it here though I'm going to get a partial. I'm happy about that it just takes like six months to get it.

Anyway, I started taking GED classes. I really want to get that and after I get it I'm going to take college courses. I'm also still working in the main kitchen. I cook for this whole prison and the prison that's up the hill. And it's real hot here and I hate the heat but right now it's raining on and off. I like the rain more than the heat. It sounds like you've been real busy with your book being released and all and you've been traveling a lot too.

I talked to my brother and he says he wants to read your book and he told me to tell you to text him because he wants to talk to you.

Anyway, I hope I hear back from you soon. Take care.

Love,
Jorge

November 3, 2016

Hi Jorge,

I hope you are doing OK. I got sick for a while and just slept a lot. It felt like a huge waste of time but I guess it's necessary. What do you do if you get sick there? Do they let you rest or keep you on work duty? I bet sicknesses spread really fast with so many people in one area.

Have you gotten letters from anyone except me and Emily?

Did you get my visiting form? I sent it a while ago so if you didn't get it, it may be lost.

What else… Have you been studying? Reading? I find that reading helps me pass time the best, but I don't know if it's like that for you. What have you liked reading the most?

I hope the weather change is good for you. Not so hot at least! I don't like the cold and rain because it makes me feel so lazy and sometimes depressed. But at least California isn't that bad.

I hope you're doing well. I am praying for you.

Love,
Ms. Harris

November 14, 2016

Dear Jorge,

I think I can come visit on December 10th! My friend Mitali will come with me if her paperwork got approved. Can you check? And we can bring Luis if he's free.

What times are visiting hours again? Mitali has to be somewhere by 4:00, but we'll figure it out. So unless I get sick again or something (I do work with children), I'll see you December 10th! I'm really looking forward to it.

Let me know if there's anything I need to know.

I saw Luis today, which was so nice. I'm glad we're all back in touch.

Love,
Miss Harris

(more later)

November 23, 2016

Hi Ms. Harris,

I'm happy to hear from you. Sorry to hear you got sick. What did you have? I haven't got sick here yet but I'm pretty sure you still have to work unless you have a doctor's note saying he gave you a lay-in.

No, I haven't gotten any letters from no one but you and Emily. I've been reading. I read that *Harry Potter* book and I just started reading your book. So far I like it. Once I'm done with it, I'll let you know what I think of the whole book.

I like that it isn't that hot no more. I hate the heat and I love the rain. I also feel lazy on rainy days sometimes too and sleepy. Dec 10th sounds good but there's only visits on weekends so if the 10th is on a Saturday or Sunday then it's all right. Your friend Mitali got approved also so both you guys can come. Visits are from 8:00 AM to 2:00 PM. When you come up here though, right before you come in there's a card you can buy for you to put money on so you can buy food out of the vending machines once you're inside. There's also coins that you can buy. I think they're two dollars for pictures and I think the food card costs five dollars. You can call my brother and have him explain it better to you.

My brother also told me you guys went out to eat. He also said you gave him your book too. He said he had a good time. Anyway, by the time you write me back I'll be done with your book so I'll give you feedback on it.

Talk to you soon. Take care. Happy Thanksgiving!

Love,
Jorge

November 30, 2016

Dear Jorge,

So, I was kind of thinking that maybe at some point we should write a book about you and your family (no real names). People need to know how hard it was for young single mothers, immigrants, etc. Let me know what you think. It's important to hear more voices, not just the voices in power.

You always tried to do the right thing when you were a kid, and you were set up to fail in a lot of ways. I'm not saying you didn't ever make bad decisions. But all the times you needed help, the adults didn't know how to help or weren't around for it. You deserved better.

I sent you a journal so you can keep a record of what's going on or work through some of your feelings. I think it helps.

My handwriting is getting worse and worse, I'm sorry!

It was fun to see Luis. Maybe I can get him to come visit, too. You'll like Mitali. She writes young adult novels about kids in different countries, and she's a really lovely person.

I'm still nervous about what you think of my book. I know not all the stuff about you was positive, but none of us are all positive and you really had it rough. I wanted to tell the truth so we can get people to change things. But I hope I was respectful because you're very important to me.

I'll see you Saturday, December 10th!

Love,
Ms. Harris

December 8, 2016

Hi Ms. Harris,

That sounds like a good idea. It'll be nice to let people know how it was for me, my brother, my mom, and my grandma living in Oakland and how hard it is to be out here as an immigrant also. That would be something big and different for me but I would like to let my mom's voice be heard to let people know how much of a good, loving mom she was and how much she tried to do her best for us.

I read your book and I loved everything about it. I think you did a great job. Everything you wrote in that book was real. When I read the chapter you wrote about me it made me realize a lot about my life. I am sitting here and thinking of how it was for me growing up and I can see it like it was just yesterday. I feel like it went by so fast. The thing I hate most was I had to be locked up when my mom passed. I know I'm not an angel. I probably did some bad things in my life to deserve it but sometimes I feel like I didn't deserve it, does that make sense? But you know life can be unfair sometimes.

I'm not sure if I can get journals. Maybe if you send it through Amazon I can get it. We'll see if I get it. I would like a journal too because sometimes I feel like writing how I feel, you know?

I'll talk to my brother so he can come with you one of these days. I'm sure he would. It's going to be nice seeing you again. By the time you get this letter you probably already came up here but if not I look forward to seeing you Saturday, I'll be ready :)

Talk to you soon.

Love,
Jorge

December 19, 2016

Dear Jorge,

Your grandma asked Luis to ask me to come over to pray the rosary for your mom on the 28th. I wish you could be there, of course, but I hope it is encouraging and comforting to know that we will be praying. And you can pray at the same time if not the same place.

I've been trying to get Luis to get his driver's license, because I worry about what could happen if he gets pulled over by the wrong cop. He keeps telling me he doesn't have time, but he needs to plan ahead, make an appointment, etc. I don't know if he'll listen to you. Do you think so?

I'm so glad so many people are writing to you! This might sound silly but don't fall in love with any of them. It's really easy to feel lonely and isolated but I am absolutely confident there's someone for you to start a family with when you're out. I know it.

You may have already written back to me about this but let me know if it's safer (just in things not being lost if you get moved) if you want to send me writings about your life and your mom's. Like maybe I could ask you one question in each letter that you could write about on a separate piece of paper and I can save them and start typing a manuscript.

Also, and this is up to you, if you want me to get some of your stories out now, I have a blog. So if you're OK with it, I could share some of your memories and stories and get people to want to know your story.

I'm praying for you this month. I know it's hard with the anniversary. Pray in any way you can—in your head, talking, writing, drawing, even yelling at God. God can handle it!

Love,
Ms. Harris

To start writing, what if you write whatever you want about either of these:
- What do you know about when your mom was a little girl?
- What are some happy memories from when you were little?

December 21, 2016

Hi Ms. Harris,

Sorry I didn't write you back right away. I just been going through some things but I'm all right. By the way, I like the Christmas card with our class picture from third grade. I don't remember that day, but I do recognize people in the card though.

I was happy to see you too! I was very nervous to see you too because it's been a long time since I saw you and you know, seeing you while I'm locked up was just weird. I had a good time though. Mitali was pretty cool too. I didn't mind that you brought her. It's always nice to meet new people.

I got the *Harry Potter* books two and three tell your sister and niece I said thank you I really appreciate it and that I wish them a Merry Christmas and a Happy New Year. I also got this book or more like a guide/journal type thing and I got the cursive book but I don't know who sent those. Oh and the journal you sent me I couldn't get it because it needs to be sent from an approved vendor, so they told me to send it to my address and I sent it to my grandma's house. She said she got it already too.

The card with the dogs looks pretty nice. They all look like they're having a bad day. Yes, I did get the stamps, thank you.

I have changed a lot for the better, but I just hate what happened to my mom. It gets me mad when I think about it. That's why I try not to, but I'll get through it. I'm just happy I have people supporting me. I also got some Christmas cards from your friends.

Anyway, I'm going to send you a Christmas card. You might get it late but you'll get it. I hope you enjoy your Christmas and New Year, take care.

Talk to you soon.

Love,
Jorge

December 28, 2016

Dear Jorge,

I went to your mom's memorial and service today. It was really nice of your grandma to invite me and she also gave me tamales. I forgot to give her the card for money for food for you, so I'll send it in the mail. It was good to see her again, but I know it was a really sad day for her and you also.

Your grandma let me take a picture of your mom's memorial altar, so I'll get it printed for you and send it when I can. What did you do today? I'm sure it was hard. I've been praying for you and Luis and your grandma all day. Anniversaries of deaths are really hard.

You said you were going through some things. What's going on? I can understand that reconnecting with someone from inside prison would be difficult. Is there anyone else you've reconnected with or no?

It's New Year's Eve right now and I have a cold, so I'm not doing anything. It's been a weird year this year, with a break-up and a couple of old friends dying and some other stuff. I would be excited about 2017 except for President Trump. I can't believe he got elected!

Are you setting any New Year's resolutions? It sounds like you kind of already have made a lot of changes in your life that took a lot of courage. That is impressive. Did I give you some questions to start writing about your life? You only have to do a tiny tiny bit at a time. Let me know if you want some questions to get you started.

OK, let me know how the new year is treating you. I'm sure you have been having a rough time with the anniversary of your mom's death, as anyone would. But it's harder when you can't be with your family at that time. I've been praying for you, and I hope God gave you some comfort. You deserved more people to help you in your life, but I hope that you can feel that God is with you. It's not easy.

Love,
Ms. Harris

January 2, 2017

Hi Ms. Harris,

I appreciate you going to my mom's memorial. It means a lot. I bet the food was good huh? You know you didn't have to give the card to my grandma, you could have saved it for next time you came but it's all right.

My grandma told me you took pictures of the memorial so I can't wait to see them. I didn't do anything on the 28th. I just stayed in the cell and I didn't want to be around nobody. So far I haven't reconnected with no one else but you.

It must have sucked to have a cold on New Year's Eve. This year was a crazy year for me too. A break up that's new, well, at least to me it is because since I've known you you've never talked about having a boyfriend and I never seen you with anybody back then. Sorry to hear about your friend's passing, it must be hard for you right now.

The New Year's resolution I have so far is to lose some weight and get my GED. That's about it for right now. Yes, you did give me some questions to start off with. I haven't started yet but I promise I'm going to start working on it.

I got those pictures you sent me too. Thank you, I'm happy I got those pics. I hope you come to visit again, I can't wait to see you. So far 2017 is good and I hope it stays like that the whole year.

Anyway, talk to you soon.

Take care.

Love,
Jorge

January 4, 2017

Hi Ms. Harris,

Yeah, my grandma told me that she asked Luis to tell you to go over there on the 28th. I wish I could have been there but I'm just happy there were people there remembering my mom.

Luis told me that you asked him to get his driver's license and that you told him you would even help pay for it but I don't know why he doesn't want to do it. I've been telling him to get it but he doesn't listen to me. I be trying to tell him things but you know there's only so much I can really do from in here. He'll learn.

It's all right, the way you said you'd just ask me a question every time you write me and I'll write about it. It's better like that.

Let me think about that blog thing. I'll get back to you on that.

Anyway, I hope you have a fun Christmas and a Happy New Year. I hope this year brings you nothing but positive things.

When I'm done writing about those two questions you asked me I'll send it. Take care.

Love,
Jorge

February 21, 2017

Dear Jorge,

How are you doing? I'm visiting a friend in San Diego and working out of her office today. It was supposed to be sunny, and it's been rainy and overcast the whole time. Oh well.

Mitali and I were thinking of visiting you on Saturday, April 1st. Would that work for you? I don't know if it's better for us to come on the same day as your grandma and give her a ride, or if you'd rather have us come on a different day. So let me know if April 1st works.

How's the weather for you? Any word on the GED class? What have you been reading lately? I've been reading one book about empathy—the ability to feel for other people. It can be a great thing, obviously, because it's good to know what other people are going through and understand them. But it can also be really harmful because you can get absolutely exhausted because it's just too much to take on everyone's feelings all the time. Like the difference between feeling a little sad for someone else's bad news and feeling their sadness as if it were your own. It was an interesting book.

There have been a lot of protests against Trump lately. I went to one protest here in San Diego. It was in support of immigrants and wanting rights for undocumented immigrants. There were 10,000 people at this march!

How are you doing in general? I know you don't really feel like you were a drug addict necessarily, but I do have some friends and family who have really liked the 12-step programs and felt like it helped them a lot. You said you've been to some in Spanish but you didn't feel comfortable? Do you think it might be a good thing in general even if you're uncomfortable, or do you feel like it doesn't apply to you?

OK, I will talk to you more when I get home. Let me know about April 1st!

Love,
Ms. Harris

March 6, 2017

Hi Ms. Harris,

Thank you for the card. It's pretty nice. I bet that mummy museum is cool. Yeah, I'm getting a lot of letters. Some of them I don't write back right away. Only you and Emily is who I write back right away. I haven't yet started writing about me and my mom's life. I think I'm going to start in April if that's cool with you because you know this month is my mom's birthday and I can't really focus right now.

April 1st sounds like a good day for you guys to come visit. It would be nice if you came by yourself one time you know.

The GED thing is going kinda slow because I only go to school once a week but I am working on it. Right now I'm reading a book Emily sent me called *Beyond Religion* and it's pretty good. I've been seeing a lot of things going on with Trump on the news like every day, it's crazy.

Right now I'm actually going to two groups, one called AA and the other CGA. The first one is for alcoholics and the other one is called Criminals and Gangmembers Anonymous. They're both good. So far I been good though staying out of trouble.

I have somebody making you a keychain. He should be done with it soon probably by the time you write me back I'll have it. Anyway, hope to talk to you soon, take care.

Love,
Jorge

March 9, 2017

Dear Jorge,

Thanks for the letter! We'll see you Saturday, April 1st then. I'll tell Luis but if you can also tell your grandma, that would be great. I think she likes to go on her own, so just make sure she knows we'll be there that day. If she wants a ride, I'd be happy to give one to her, but I do think she likes to see you with just family.

I will totally come on my own someday! It's tough because my back hurts if I drive for too long. But Mitali also said she can leave partway through the visit and give us some time together. Would you like that?

Remember, you don't have to write to anyone you don't want to! Only if it's bringing you joy. I understand about your mom. What day is her birthday? Of course you can start writing in April. Maybe spend thirty minutes every day writing about her and your life. I think you'd be really surprised how much you can do in thirty minutes a day but being disciplined is hard. Just remember how important it is for other people to learn about your life as well as your mom's.

So which day of the week is the GED class? Does it feel hard or easy to you? Do they have a good teacher?

I agree that Trump is crazy. I hope that someday we will learn to treat everyone in America with respect, whether they're undocumented or not.

Do you like AA or GCA better or the two about the same? Are you meeting friends in there? I know some of those programs can help you get close to God, and I like how they phrase it—the God of your understanding. We all understand God totally differently, and I think that's OK because God is a huge mystery that I don't think we can fully understand in this life. That book Emily sent you seems interesting.

Also, I think it's OK to think about all sides. Some people want to disprove that there is a God. I've seen God take care of too many people in my life, so I believe. But I don't usually understand God, you know?

For example, I think it's a huge miracle that you left the gang. But I'm angry that you had a hard life in the first place. I know God helps us, but I don't know why God allows suffering at all. Does that make sense?

I hope you have a good week.

Love,
Ms. Harris

April 10, 2017

Dear Jorge,

How are you doing? It was really good to see you last weekend. It was nice of Mitali to give us some time on our own, too. You looked better than last time; I'm hoping you're feeling more optimistic, but I'm sure it can be hard.

What did you think of her idea about making a book out of our letters? You would get to look first, of course, and take out anything you're not comfortable with, but I think it could be a really good idea. I'd love for people to see that just because you're in prison does not mean you're anything other than a wonderful person who made some bad choices and didn't have the opportunities many others had.

It got cold and rainy here again this week, which is not my favorite. I think you don't like hot weather, so maybe this is better for you.

If you let me know the names of the other prisons you're thinking about requesting, I can check distances for you if you want. Was your auntie able to come visit?

How's the writing going? I've been procrastinating a lot. Sometimes it's hard to write every day. But just like I tell you, you just have to do it. I do, too. Sometimes for me writing feels really energizing, and sometimes it's just exhausting.

How is the reading? Let me know when you have room for more Harry Potter books! I'm glad so many people have been sending you books. Hopefully it's a good visual reminder of how important you are—even to people who have only just read about you! And, of course, if they're not interesting to you or you're done with them you can give them away.

I'm sending a copy of our picture and a printout explaining the Stanford Prison experiment. I am not positive they'll let you receive printouts like this, so let me know if you get it.

If you're interested in doing the book with our letters, a good first step would be to send me back the letters I wrote to you. I can always make copies and send them back to you if you want them. I will start making copies now of the letters I write. I just don't want anything to get lost if you move or anything. Let me know your thoughts.

And remember, there are a lot of people thinking about you and praying for you.

Love,
Ms. Harris

(You can call me Bronwyn if you want! My rule for former students is that as soon as they turn 18, they can use my first name if they want.)

April 23, 2017

Hi Bronwyn :),

It was nice seeing you again. Yeah it was nice of Mitali to give us some time alone. I do feel better than last time.

I think Mitali's idea is pretty good. I would like to look at them first though. It did rain for a couple days over here but then it stopped. I like the rain but not while I'm locked up. My auntie was not able to come but my grandma said they're coming next week.

I've been procrastinating but I wrote something that I'm sending you with this letter. Let me know if I did good. You can ask me some questions so I can keep writing. The reading is going good. I'll let you know when I'm ready for some more books.

I did get the picture and the printout. I'm going to gather all the letters and see how I can send all of them at one time. Let me know what you think about what I wrote. Take care.

Love,
Jorge

April 29, 2017

Dear Jorge,

I hope your auntie and your grandma were able to visit since I've last heard from you! I wish I could visit more often. I've been working way too much, and I'm generally super busy. It's good to have the work so I can save money, but it's hard to find a good balance of making money and having time to myself, too. Is it hard to constantly be around people and not be able to have time for yourself?

I wanted to get an answer to you quickly, but I'm taking more time now and reading the beginning of your life story again. It is incredibly powerful. I'm really thankful that you're willing to share this because people need to know what life is like for other people, not just themselves. And especially because you had so many hard things happen when you were just a kid. I think that as a whole, our society really should have done better by you. I wish we had.

Your writing is honest, and that is the most powerful thing of all. If you're willing, I'll share the beginning or certain quotes on my blog and my author Facebook page. We have time, but I'd love to build up an audience so that when we do write it people will be interested. But I won't do it without your permission, so let me know.

I know I gave you a bunch of questions in the other card, but here's another one: Why are you willing to write about your life? What makes it important for you to tell this story?

Tomorrow I'm taking my four-year-old nephew to San Francisco. He really really wanted to go on a boat, so for his birthday we're taking the ferry. I'll get to see my brother and sister-in-law and little niece (she's almost two) also, and then he and I will go on the boat alone. He's pretty excited!

I know you can understand this—the doctor is changing my antidepressants around (you're not the only one who's had to take them), so it's kind of messing with me and making me not sleep, etc. Did you go totally off the medication?

Good job on the writing. I'm proud of you!

—Bronwyn/Ms. Harris

May 17, 2017

Hi Bronwyn,

How are you?

Well my grandma came to see me this past weekend and she wanted me to ask you for a favor, something she needs help with. She told me she has been going to the Oakland police department asking for the paperwork on my mom's death and they keep telling her that they don't have nothing on record for a death on that date or that name. I don't really understand how they don't have any of that on file you know. I'm going to give you her number so you can call her and she can explain what she wants to do. I'm almost done answering one of those questions. Once I'm done I'll send it, okay?

Take to you soon.

Take care.

Love,
Jorge

May 22, 2017

Dear Jorge,

I have so much work this week that this'll be quick, but wanted to answer your questions. I can ask around for how to get files from the Oakland Police. They're supposed to be more helpful if it's a family member, but obviously it's not working. Can you tell me exactly what she's looking for? Is it the police report, fire report, or death report? That will tell me if it's the police dept, fire dept, or coroner. If it's the coroner, they probably won't tell anyone who's not family, my reporter friend tells me. (It's the same reporter friend that helped me find you at your first prison!) Let me know.

I don't have your grandma's number or Luis's new number. If you can get me those, it would be good. And I know I know where she lives, but I can't remember the exact address.

One question for you: Do you still have a lawyer? Or do you have the information of the lawyer you had? I love the idea of publishing your writing, but I want to run it by a lawyer to make sure it doesn't hurt you at all for parole or anything. I don't see why it would, but I want to absolutely make sure.

OK, more later, but I didn't want to make you wait!

Bronwyn

June 2, 2017

Jorge—another quick note—I got your writing, and it's great! Just keep getting the things out of your mind, and we'll organize later. Do you need more topics? Let me know and I'll write more questions.

I met a lawyer today who told me he thinks it's fine if you publish while you're in, but he's going to check to make sure! We can also use a pseudonym if that's more comfortable. But if you still have a lawyer, we can check with them too.

Keep writing. You're doing GREAT!

—Bronwyn

June 7, 2017

Hi Bronwyn,

Yeah my auntie and grandma came last Saturday with my brother. It was good to see my auntie, you know, after a long time. I can only imagine how it is on the streets[5] because I go through the same thing in here. I work all morning then after work I have to work out by the time I'm done working out I feel all tired. Then I shower take a nap and wake up so I can finish off what I have to do. Yeah, it does suck not being able to have time for yourself.

I'm glad you liked what I wrote. I already wrote down all the questions you asked me on this letter and the card you sent me. I'll start answering them one by one when I'm done with one I'll send it to you. If you want you can post things on your blog it's not a problem. Just let me know what you post. You can also show Mitali what I wrote.

I'm going to ask somebody how I can send you all the letters at one time. Once I find out I'll let you know.

That's good I'm pretty sure your nephew will have lots of fun because I know every time you and Mr. Jackson took me and my brother out, I always had fun.

I didn't know you take meds. They took me all the way off my meds because I wasn't going to take them anymore. I'm doing good without them really.

I liked the dog pictures too. They look like they're having fun. Anyway hope to hear from you soon. When I'm done with the writing I'll send it. Take care.

Love,
Jorge

---

5 Here, Jorge means "not in prison," as opposed to homeless.

June 14, 2017

Hey Bronwyn,

I'm happy to hear you're going to Scotland. I'm pretty sure you're going to have a great time. I'd love to get postcards or pictures. The writing is going good, but every time I write it just makes me think about everything I've been through and everything from when I started gangbanging until now and you know everything about my mom also. I talked to my grandma and she told me she wanted the report of my mom's death but when she went to the police department asking for it they told her there is not a death report for a person in that name and they don't have anything on record for a death in that area where she died or date. She even showed them the newspaper where it showed her death and they still said they had nothing. You can call her. You can also send me some more questions to write on.

Have you heard anything about Emily? I haven't heard from her in a while. I just wrote her too like last week. Anyway, have fun in Scotland and take care. Hope to hear from you soon.

Love,
Jorge

June 15, 2017

Dear Jorge,

This will be quick because I'm about to go on vacation tomorrow, so I have to pack! I can send you a postcard if you want; I will probably send it when I get back, though, because I'm not sure if I can send anything to you from another country.

I'm really excited to go to Scotland, although an eleven-hour flight does *not* sound fun to me at all! But I have two friends I can sit by on the plane to pass the time.

I don't have your grandma or brother's phone numbers, so can you send those to me? Or you can just tell Luis to text me. Did your grandma figure out the police records at all?

I hope you're doing OK and that it's not too hot. What are you reading these days? How is the writing going?

I'll be in touch when I get back in a couple weeks.

Love,
Bronwyn

July 3, 2017

Dear Jorge,

I just got back from Scotland! I wrote you a postcard but then I left it with a friend who is still there so I will mail it when she comes back and gives it back to me. Also, I think today is your birthday, and I'm really sorry I was gone and couldn't send you a birthday card on time. So maybe I'll send you a couple, and we can just make July your birthday month. :)

Scotland was really beautiful. Very green and relaxing, with lots and lots of sheep. I've been reading some books that are a little silly but also really good (a time travel romance for one—told you it sounded silly) that are set there, so I've learned a lot about the history of Scotland and how they were taken over by the English. There was a lot of killing.

I hope your birthday is/was OK. I'm sure spending special days inside is probably pretty hard. Are you twenty-two now?

I will get in touch with your grandma as soon as I can. I am exhausted from the trip and trying to catch up on two weeks of work, but it's on my list. Can you give me Luis's number too? The one I have for him doesn't work.

Your writing is going great from what I see. Is it hard to do? I mean, not the writing, because you're writing well, but emotionally. I'm hoping it feels healing but I know it might also bring up a lot of things that are hard to feel. I really think you have to feel them before you can heal though.

I just got a new housemate who is pretty great and has a little dog, so the two dogs are friends—at least so far). I'd rather live by myself, but it's just so expensive that I can't do it. I'm trying to save up money, so I have to work a lot and have roommates. I really really want to get out to visit you again soon but I've been working a lot of weekends. It'll happen, I promise. I just don't know when.

What's the summer like there? I'm sure it's super hot, and I'm sure it's much harder to deal with a lot of people in the heat. I hope that doesn't get too hard, but I'm guessing there's a lot of times when it's really hard to calm down or walk away, or just that you suffer, from not having alone time. I hope writing can help some. I hear meditation helps, but I don't know so much about it.

Do you need any more books?

Let me know how you're doing!

Love,
Bronwyn

July 4, 2017

Dear Jorge,

HAPPY BIRTHDAY! I know I'm late. But I believe in celebrating your whole birthday month. There's not much I can send you for your birthday but if you want photos of Scotland, or a book or... can I send you colored pencils or pens from Amazon or no?

Emily said something happened that you have to stay in your cell more. What happened?

I'm so glad you're telling your story.

Love,
Bronwyn

July 14, 2017

Hi Bronwyn,

I'm happy to hear you're back from Scotland. Glad you had a good time out there. I bet it was really nice. Why was there a lot of sheep? Is Scotland known for sheep or something?

My birthday was all right. I really didn't do nothing, you know, you really don't celebrate birthdays in prison. I'm just happy I'm twenty-two now.

The writing is kind of hard in certain ways but it's alright. I know I haven't wrote anything in a while but I promise I'll get back on it.

That's cool that you got a roommate, to save money. It's cool you know but it's always better to live by yourself.

Summers over here kind of sucks because it gets real real hot but other than that it's all right. And to be honest I haven't really been getting mad. I really don't even get mad at all no more so that's good.

Other than that though I been good. Right now I don't need any books because I still have a whole bunch of books. I'm almost done with this book called *Tuesdays with Morrie* then I'll probably read the Cesar Chavez book.

I would like pictures from Scotland if you don't mind. I will be sending you some writing soon okay. Take care.

Love,
Jorge

July 23, 2017

Hi Ms. Harris,

I'm stuck in the cell so I'm bored and felt like writing you. I would be writing about my life story but I need some more questions. I don't think I told you why I can't come out the cell as much so I'm going to tell you.

Well, you know when I got to this prison I was borderline level four, so in the beginning of this year I got two write-ups like two months from each other. So I ended up doing thirty days loss of yard for the first write-up and the second one so in total I did sixty days loss of yard.

For each write-up you get six points, so my annual just passed this June. Once a year you go to committee, so when I went they told me that I recently got two serious write-ups so my points went from fifty-eight to sixty-four which is level four. So they had to send me to a level four and they put me on C-status for four months.

What C-status means is that you can only come out the cell Monday through Friday for two hours, you can't come out on holidays or weekends, you can't get no packages, and my program is just hella strict. I been on C-status for a month and one week so far. I also got moved to A-yard which is a level four. I got a better celly than I had over there though. I get off C-status October 11th so I'm trying to do good.

Anyway, guess what: I'm going to cut my hair off. I think it's about that time to go back to short hair.

I also wanted to ask you if you think you can send me copies of the things I wrote about so far and when you write me back send me some more questions. Talk to you soon. Take care.

Love,
Jorge

July 27, 2017

Hey Bronwyn,

Well, I got transferred to another prison on Tuesday. It kind of sucks but you know I really can't do nothing about it. I guess they played me when I went to committee because I was supposed to be endorsed to the level four at the other prison which is A-yard. I was only on that yard for two weeks then they moved me over to this new place. I'm on a level four yard right now but I really don't know where this prison is by. I'm good I just wrote you this quick letter so you can know what's going on and so you can have the address to this prison so you can write me over here. Anyway take care. Hope to hear from you soon.

Love,
Jorge

July 28, 2017

Dear Jorge,

Sorry for the delay in writing. I got a bunch of work, which was really good because I really needed the money, but I don't have a lot of control over when the work comes in sometimes, being self-employed.

Scotland is kind of known for sheep, I guess. I don't know that much about sheep, but maybe it's because it rains a lot, so they get a lot of grass and sheep eat grass? Just a guess! Sheep are funny. They're really dumb (but cute) so the sheepdogs totally work. I mean, the dogs can make the sheep do just about anything they want even though the sheep are bigger and there's way more of them. They eat them and also make a ton of yarn and fabric out of the wool. I like wool because it's warm and you know I like to knit, but the yarn there was all really expensive and really scratchy. I liked the little sheep's faces though. If you want any photos, let me know! I'll get them eventually…

Yeah, I think I would like to live by myself but this new roommate is turning out to be really good. She's really positive and generous and our dogs get along well. So, while I always wish I could afford to live alone, it's nice to have someone right there to be able to talk to when I'm working out an issue or someone made angry or whatever.

One of the big things I'm working on, just as a person, is realizing when something is someone else's problem and they're trying to make it mine. You know what I mean? Like when someone takes out their anger or fear or something on me, and I automatically react, either by arguing with them or just feeling really bad or anxious. And talking it through sometimes makes me realize that it's just 100% their problem and I can walk away. I mean, that's over-simplifying it a lot, but I'm trying to not let other people affect me as much. I'm sure that's easier for me when I don't have to be around other people all the time like you do, though.

Remember when I used to tell my students that when people were mean, it was because they felt bad about themselves? I think it's super true about adults.

I connected with your grandma through Luis (you know my Spanish isn't good enough for all this vocabulary). Turns out the case about your mom is still "open," even though the police aren't actively investigating it. I am not sure why, but it seems to be a common thing. And they can't release any information on an open case. I'll keep trying them every few months and eventually we'll get more information, but it'll be a while.

You said you don't really get mad any more. How did that happen? I do remember you having a temper for sure when you were younger. Tell me more if you feel about it.

How was *Tuesdays with Morrie*? I haven't read it. Let me know if there are ever any books you want us both to read and talk about.

I do remember that you were borderline between two levels and I'm sorry that you got write-ups and lost yard time. Sorry to hear also that you went to C-status. Can you still get visitors? Emily and I are trying to figure out when we can come. And I know Mitali wants to come back too. I want to come by myself, too, but they both want me to go with them and I'm trying to balance all the work. So if you want me to ask either of them if we can have some time just ourselves too, let me know and I will. Is Emily still writing to you?

Glad you have a better celly! Does he actually shower? That bird bath thing sounded nasty. Are you in any of the 12-step groups still or doing anything else?

Sometimes it's fun to have a change in hair, I do know that! I'll send you copies of the things you wrote; give me a little time to find them. Do you want copies of the letters or just the writing about your life?

Here are some questions, and feel free to pick and choose, and ignore any you feel like you've already done.
- Describe your siblings and your relationships with them.
- Do you know anything about what your mom was like as a child?
- Do you know how your parents met?

- Do you know how your grandma and mom came into the U.S.?
- Was there ever a time in your childhood you felt like you didn't have major responsibilities? I know by the time I met you, you were taking care of a lot of people in your family. Did you ever feel like you just got to be a kid or no because of where and how you grew up?
- What was it like to go to kindergarten?

And of course anything else you think of!

I'll write more soon and try to get photos for you.

Love,
Bronwyn

August 2, 2017

Hi Bronwyn,

Don't worry about the delay. I got transferred anyway. I'm glad you got the new address before you wrote me back because if not it would have took three weeks for me to get your letter because of reroute.

That's funny how you said sheep are dumb, but I've seen that on TV where the sheepdogs can make the sheep go anywhere they want. I would like to get some pictures whenever you get them.

I'm glad to hear you and your roommate are getting along well and that your dogs get along. Also I understand what you're working on. There's a lot of that that goes on in here believe it or not, it's crazy. I do remember when you used to tell us that about mean people. I believe it's true now also.

I'm happy you talked to my grandma about that situation with my mom. I think it's kind of stupid though that my mom's case is still open but they're not investigating. Makes no sense.

Yes, I don't get mad no more like that. I don't know how it happened but it did. I guess it might be because of being locked up, because when I first got locked up, I used to get mad at a lot of things. Like when I was in the county you go to breakfast at four in the morning right? Then sometimes they wake you up at 5:30 to go to court and they put you in a holding cell with hella people but they don't come and get you till like 8:00. I used to get mad at that a lot.

Then being in prison, I learned to have patience for a lot of things. I guess that's one of the main reasons why I don't get mad any more. I just want to get out and be able to be like this on the street.

I still can get visits on C-status. But I'm kind of mad I got moved to this prison because I know it's a lot more further from home. I might not be getting visits as much from my grandma because I'm way down here. But when I go to my annual again which is next year I'm going to ask to go somewhere like where I was. I do want to meet Emily so you know you guys can take your time and find a date that fits both you guys. I'm also sending you some visiting forms. I don't know how many you wanted, so let me know if you need more. Yes, Emily is still writing me it takes her a while to write me back but she still writes.

I like having short hair again!

Anyway, I hope to hear back from you soon. Take care.

Love,
Jorge

August 7, 2017

Dear Jorge,

Well, I'm glad you've been able to learn to have patience. That is not an easy thing to learn at all and you will be a better person if you're able to have patience, and probably happier too. It can be tough though.

I have nothing very exciting to tell you right now… I think I already told you that my dog ate a ton of chocolate, and I had to take her to the emergency vet. She's OK though.

Have you been reading any good books lately? Do they have you on work duty yet? How do you spend your days?

I will write more soon, I promise.

Love,
Bronwyn

August 15, 2017

Hey Bronwyn,

I just got done writing another piece of my life story. I wrote on the question you asked about: Describe your siblings and your relationships with them—first I wrote about Luis. I'm going to write about each brother and sister.

Well, I have good news. I went to committee last week and they decided to take me off C-status so they signed me up for school and they're putting me in the SAP program, which stands for substance abuse program. So now I can really focus on getting my GED and get some time taken off my sentence.

Who were the visiting forms for? You know you don't have to send new forms just because I got moved. Once you're approved you're approved in every prison in California. I'm pretty sure because I remember I asked somebody and they told me once you're approved you're good. The only thing is right now I don't have boots so I can't get visits. They said they ran out so I have to wait two weeks.

Last week I got moved to another building because the building I was at was an orientation and C-status building. The celly I got is an older dude but he is way better than the celly I had at the other prison.

Anyway, that's about it I'm sending you some more writing I did and take care. Talk to you soon.

Love,
Jorge

August 20, 2017

Dear Jorge,

Oh, I totally thought I had to resubmit the forms, so it was for me, Mitali, and Emily. If we just stay approved, that's fine. Just let me know!

That was some really wonderful stuff you wrote about Luis. Do you want a copy so you can send to him? Or want me to? Or would you rather he not see it yet? I'm wondering now if you've told your family you're writing your life story. If so, what do they think? Want to ask Luis to write anything too or would he not be interested?

I'm teaching a class to adults this weekend so they can pass a test to be a teacher. The test isn't that hard, but some people have test anxiety, and some don't speak English as their first language so it's harder for them to write in English. And one person in this class this time is Deaf. The school provides sign language interpreters, which is really interesting for me to watch but of course I can't watch because she's translating my talking. I do get a little distracted, but I'm really glad they give her that resource.

I don't know if you've been following the news, but there are neo-Nazis who have been protesting the removal of Confederate statues. Do you remember learning about the Civil War in fifth grade? If you don't, I'll print out some information for you or send you a book if you want because it's turning out to be super important these days. So one reason the South wanted to leave the United States was slavery, and when the Civil Rights movement started in the 1950s and 1960s to give Black and brown people more rights, that's when they started putting up the statues of the Confederate "heroes" from the Civil War a hundred years before that. And a lot of why they did it was to intimidate and scare Black people.

Now some people are realizing that maybe we don't need statues honoring people who fought against the United States for slavery, and the racists are angry. So there are all these people marching with Confederate (from the Civil War) flags and Nazi flags. I can't imagine being Jewish or Black and seeing these people and knowing that they don't think you should be free or even alive.

It's insane. I just gave a donation to the Jewish temple in my town because it got vandalized. It makes me really sad.

So you can't have visitors because you don't have boots? What do you wear on your feet? That's not fair at all. I am glad to hear you're getting off C-status, though. Is A-status the best? How far down does it go?

When do you start the GED class? Tell Luis he'd better start the process too! Maybe you'll be an inspiration to him. And the substance abuse program: Are you still having any substance abuse problems, or is this from earlier? I don't know how long you've been clean or what you were using. You don't have to tell me if you don't want.

I'm happy to help your celly if I can. It might depend on how common his friend's name is and how much she's on the internet. For example, it's easy to find me because my name is unusual and I've written a bunch of stuff on the internet. Give me whatever he knows about her: full name, what city she lives in, what languages she speaks, what prison she was translating at.

One question: You know I can't ever stop being a teacher. If you make any grammar mistakes in your letters do you want me to tell you or leave them alone? I know you didn't get as much school as you deserved, so if you want some more instruction, let me know, and if not, totally fine. :)

So, what books are you reading now? I'm reading a really creepy mystery and a silly book about art history. I know that doesn't sound like it goes together, but it's like the author made these famous painters into silly characters and they're sort of solving a mystery. It's much funnier than the other mystery I'm reading.

Let me know about visiting. My weekends are totally full until October, which I don't like but it's how it is. Some of the stuff is good though: I'm going to San Diego to visit a friend, and I'm throwing an anniversary party for my parents. But I know Mitali wants to come down maybe in November or December. She's grieving her dad's death; you know how that is. And Emily and I want to find a time, too. Obviously, it's a little harder since you're farther away, but we'll make it happen.

Love,
Bronwyn

August 27, 2017

Hi Bronwyn,

Yes, once you're approved you're good, so don't worry.

Thank you, and I know I could have written more about him but I want to write a whole page front and back about each of my brothers and sisters. As you know that might be kind of hard because I really wasn't around a few of my siblings but I'm going to write what I know.

I would like a copy of what I wrote about Luis but I want a typed copy please. If you want you can send him a copy and just let him know like: Hey your brother is writing a book about his life story and this is what he wrote about you and see if he gives you any feedback on it. The only person that knows I'm writing my life story is Luis but that's all he knows.

That's funny you're teaching adults how to be teachers. I learned how to do sign language when I was on the main line in the county, but the sign language I know is different from the one deaf people do.

I have been watching the news on the American Nazis and watching them just gets me mad, that's why I hate them racist people. I feel like Trump is the one promoting all that's been going on regarding all the racist and Nazi stuff. Also I don't remember learning about the Civil War. I would like a book on it so I can learn about it.

I also forgot to tell you that when I got here they took a lot of books from me because I guess you can only have ten books. They took books that I didn't even read yet. They even took the Bible you sent me and Mitali's book too. I still got your book though. So now what we're gonna do is once I'm done reading a book I'll let you know so you can send me a new one. If you want though you can send me that Bible again.

You only wear boots to visits or for certain jobs, but in here you have regular shoes that you buy off the packages. They have all kinds of shoes: Nikes,

Jordans, Reeboks, they have damn near everything. They put me on the list for school. Once there is an opening they'll put me in. I was having substance abuse problem. That's why I got those write-ups, 'cause I was drinking. But I haven't lately and believe me I don't want to go back on C-status. Other than that I been clean from everything else since I been locked up. On the streets I was doing everything except heroin and all that. I started when I was thirteen or fourteen.

LOL! That's funny. Sure Ms. Harris, I don't mind you can tell me if I make any grammar mistakes. Right now I'm reading a book about Cesar Chavez. Emily sent it to me. It's pretty good you know to learn about what he stood for.

Well, I hope you have fun in San Diego, and whenever you guys figure out a date to come see me let me know I'll be here. Mitali did tell me what happened to her dad that's messed up. I know how she feels. My prayers go out to her and her family.

Talk to you soon, take care.

Love,
Jorge

September 2, 2017

Hi Jorge,

OK, thanks for letting me know about the visiting! They sent me an email saying that my "preferred prison" (which was a strange way of saying it) was the old one, so will you double check just to make sure?

Here are two things: Your words about Luis for one and also a story about you that I just got accepted into a book. Have you ever heard of the *Chicken Soup for the Soul* books? They're kind of sappy and cheesy but sometimes they have OK stories and they're all about a theme. Like *Chicken Soup for the Teenage Soul* or *Chicken Soup for the Fathers*. (They might have a one for prisoners actually if you want it, let me know). So they're doing one about "stepping outside of your comfort zone" and I wrote something up really quick about visiting you, and they're publishing it! So I've sent you the story. I'll get you the book in October-ish when it's out if you want! It doesn't pay me much, but it's a real book that people know so it's exciting!

As far as the book of our letters, do you still have the ones from me, or did they take them away? I have all yours at least.

I love that you're going to keep writing about your family. I'll tell you, I don't know if we'll make any money off the book but I'm so glad you're going to do it. It is really validating and it will be so important for you to be able to teach people who only know one way of life. I'm certainly HOPING you'll make money but I haven't off my other book yet. But it's OK, it'll happen. I hope people will be open to hearing what you have to say. It might take years, but people *need* to know. Thank you for doing this. When it gets closer we'll talk about how to publish it, how you get paid, etc. But there's a lot of just hard work that needs to happen before that. I think you're ready for hard work, though.

Yeah, I liked teaching the adults but I prefer kids. The adults were from a bunch of different countries: China, Singapore, Mexico, India, and I can't remember where else. They're all trying to be teachers, but they don't all have great English so it's hard. I hope I was helpful for them.

I agree with you that Trump is promoting this stuff. He's very hateful and doesn't think about anyone except himself. I think there's probably actually something wrong with him. Even more than him, the people who maybe aren't crazy but horribly greedy and selfish make me furious. I have to take breaks from the news because I get so angry and sad.

I'm happy to get you a Civil War book. I might get a kids' one, like 4th–7th grade level, just because the adult ones can be super boring, but let me know if you'd rather have a adult one. Often when I am trying to learn history I read the kids' books.

I'll send you the Bible now. Let me know when you finish another book and what you'd like sent, OK?

I'm sorry you were drinking, but I know it can be hard to stop on your own. I know many people who have been through the 12 steps. Most of them it's really helped. I hope whatever program you do not only helps you with that but also just with dealing with any of the difficult feelings that make someone want to use or drink. Do you think it was harder to stop drugs since you started so young? I hope they get you into the GED class soon! You're so smart. You definitely deserve an education.

I'm glad you're learning about Cesar Chavez! Did you learn anything totally new to you? What will you read next?

I'll send you a postcard from San Diego if you want. Unfortunately, I can't find your friend's name online, because it's such a common name that there are a million of them. I wish Luis would just help you, and his girlfriend could relax! He told me that his girlfriend was jealous that I took him out to lunch once, and I was like, "I am older than your mom would be, she needs to chill." As for your friend, I can ask around with former students I'm still in touch with, but no promises.

Well, I hope this didn't get too long. Thanks for letting me correct your grammar if need be. Only minor things here: "A lot" is two words not one, which *nobody* can remember. See, I'm still your teacher!! Oh, and do you know the difference between "you're" and "your"? If not let me know and I'll explain it; it came up when I was teaching adults because they were super confused.

Love,
Bronwyn

PS—I see they changed you to D instead of C, is that better or worse?
Also, I called you "Jorge" in the story, just like in my book. Just for your privacy.

September 12, 2017

Hi Bronwyn,

I'm going to request a list of all the people that's approved to come visit me. Once I get it back I'll let you know.

Ok, so I read that story you wrote about me and I loved it. I've never heard of those *Chicken Soup for the Soul* books. Are you going to have to write more or is that one story going to be the whole book? I would like to read the book once it's out.

I do still have all your letters. Next time I go to the store I'm going to buy a big manila envelope and send you a couple letters. If it works, I'll just send them to you that way.

I like that I'm writing about me and my family too. Also I really don't care if I make money off it. If I do then good, if I don't then still good. I just want to show people there's not just one way of life, and just to be able to put my life story on paper like that is great.

Well, if you think I'll learn better off the kids' book just send me that one. I'll let you know once I get the Bible and I'll also let you know when I'm done reading another book. I'm almost done with the Cesar Chavez book. I learned a lot by reading that book, it's crazy. I'm probably going to read the Nelson Mandela book next.

I don't consider myself an alcoholic but I like drinking. Sometimes I choose to do it, I know it's not right and that it gets me in trouble but I'm done with drinking. I'm not getting in trouble for something petty like that. I guess you can say it's harder to stop using when you start young but being locked up it's easier to not use then it would be if you were on the streets.

I can't wait until they put me in the GED class either. I don't know why it's taking so long. I feel like the longer it takes for them to put me in school the longer it's going to take for me to get my GED.

Thank you for getting that address for my celly and he also says thank you. Hopefully he gets in contact with her.

Yeah, you can send me a postcard from San Diego if you like.

That sucks that you couldn't find my friend. Thanks for trying

Anyway about the grammar, I did think a lot was one word not two. OK so tell me if I'm right, you're is short for you are and your is like saying I'm going to your house or its basically like something that you own. Let me know if I'm correct.

By the way, do you think you can send me some binder paper because I only got like two pieces of paper left. That's why I haven't wrote anything about my life story. You think you can also send me a few 6 × 9 manila envelopes for some drawings?

Oh, and I don't think I ever told you that I got on that website called writeaprisoner.com. I did it myself, I just had my grandma send a $40 money order and they made me a profile. I only been on there for a month so far one girl has wrote me but she's from the UK. She's 27. I wrote her back but I'm pretty sure it's probably going to take a while since she lives in the UK. She asked me if I had email access. I told her I didn't but I'll see what happens when she writes me back.

Anyway, once again I liked that story you did. Hope to hear back from you soon. Take care.

Love,
Jorge

September 17, 2017

Dear Jorge,

Great, I'm glad you can try sending the letters. I think starting in April I started typing them so you don't have to send April or later. But if you're wanting somewhere to keep them safe, you can and I'll keep them for you. Either way.

I went through and typed all of the letters you sent me. I've noticed that you have gotten much better at writing! Even though you're not doing the GED classes yet, I think just the act of writing has made you a better writer. As you've been writing, you've gotten better at expressing yourself, and also better at paragraphs and sentences. Good job!

You're right about "you're" (short for you are) and "your" (your house). A lot of people don't know that.

I sent you some paper and envelopes from Amazon and also a book on the Civil War. I did end up getting a regular adult book because it was highly recommended, and I think you've been reading enough high-level books now that you'll be fine. But let me know if it doesn't work for you for any reason. I hope you got the Bible.

The *Chicken Soup for the Soul* books have a lot of little stories like mine in them, so there might be like twenty to forty stories in one book. I'll definitely send it to you when it comes out.

OK, another grammar correction and let me know if you don't want this, but I know you're working on writing so you probably want to sharpen your skills. Instead of "have wrote" or "haven't wrote" it's "have written" or "haven't written." If you want to know, it's the past participle, "written." Just like you'd say "have eaten" instead of "have ate." Grammar can be complicated and unfortunately boring to learn about sometimes.

I'm so glad you liked the story. I always want to be respectful when I'm writing about people, especially people who may not be able to speak for themselves at the moment for whatever reason. But you will be speaking for yourself soon enough. I am really glad you're writing your story.

I hope AA (and I forget the other group you're in) are good supports for you. Even if you're not an alcoholic, if you're used to using it to feel good or forget problems or anything it could still be hard.

I have to go now because it's a super busy week since I'm getting ready to go to San Diego for a week. Do you need more topics for your life story or no? I'll write you as soon as I'm back. Let me know if you get the paper, envelopes, and book.

Love,
Bronwyn

September 29, 2017

Hi Bronwyn,

I don't have none of my mail in order so I'm just going to send you all of it and you can just hold it for me. I also think I've gotten better on my writing. I imagine when I do start going to school, I'm probably going to get even better.

I haven't got the Bible, paper, or the Civil War book yet. I think it's because over here they have to call you to the package window to give you books and things like that. It's not like at the other prison where they just give it to you like it's mail. Plus the C.O. that works the package window takes hella long to pass things out. My last package I got took like a whole month for me to get. At the other prison it took like a week for you to get a package. But if you sent it, I'm sure I'll get it soon.

Well, I'm happy I got the "you're" and "your" thing right. I don't know how that can be confusing if you really look at it but I guess it could be. Thank you for correcting me on that "have wrote" thing. Now that I'm looking at it, it kind of makes sense. I just never really looked at it.

Yeah, I love that story you wrote. I can't wait to see it in a book. In my package I just got I bought some paper and pens so I will start writing my life story again. By the way, I'm not in any groups over here, because it's kind of hard to get in groups here. They have a long list they go by before you can get in.

I've been thinking a lot about relationships. I think a partner should make you a better person not a jealous person. I've become a great person since I been locked up so I think when I find me somebody, I'll become an even greater person but in due time it'll happen.

By the way I need some help with something if you can. When I got sentenced they gave me a $10,000 restitution for everything that was damaged in my case. So I know there's a motion that can be filed so they can either reduce it to something reasonable or just take the restitution away because there is no way I can pay that money. I've heard of people getting their restitution taken off because they had no income to pay it.

So I talked to one of my aunties and I explained to her the situation. She told me to send her the information on how to take off the restitution so she can take it to a lawyer to see what can be done. So I'm asking you if you can find me any information on how to take off the restitution so I can send it to her.

Anyway, I'm going to send you a couple of the letters you wrote me along with this letter and please let me know if you got them. If you get them then that's how I'll send them to you every time I write you back. So hope to hear back from you soon. Take care.

Love,
Jorge

October 21, 2017

Dear Jorge,

I apologize for taking so long to write back. Have you been watching those fires on the news? They got really close to my parents' and my sister's house so I've been nervous, not sleeping much, and worried that they might evacuate or lose their homes. All of them are fine, but they all have friends who have lost everything. It burned more than 3,000 homes just in the city of Santa Rosa, where my sister lives. Very scary and now there are a lot more people homeless than before. It's going to be a rough recovery.

When do you get to start your GED? I do think you'll get better and better too. Want another tip? Let me know if you don't! In Spanish, it's OK to say *no tengo nada* for example, but in English we can't say "Don't have none." It's called a double negative, just like "Don't know nobody." So that's your grammar tip for the day, it's "Don't have any," or "Don't know anybody."

Have you gotten the Civil War book or Bible yet? I sent you some envelopes and paper too. I hope they've gotten it to you.

I will send you the book as soon as it's available on Amazon. It has something like fifty stories in it, but I hope you will think mine is the best. :) I texted Luis to see if he wanted to see it but he never responded.

Let me know if you need more questions for your life story. Just keep writing and writing. The more the better.

I don't know anything about restitution but I've printed out what I can find so that you can get it to your auntie. Do you still have the same lawyer or not anymore? Was it a public defender?

I did get the letters, so that works to just mail me a few at a time.

I ran out of paper so this is being printed on scratch paper of a college class I sometimes teach. It's through a university extension and helps people pass the

CBEST, which is the test teachers need to take to get their credential. I had eleven students and I think five different languages in the class this weekend. They have to pass the test in English no matter what they are teaching, so I am really trying to help them, but they're the ones who have to take the test.

I'll try to write more next time. Keep writing about your life!

Love,
Bronwyn

October 28, 2017

Hi Bronwyn,

You don't have to apologize. You told me you were going to San Diego anyway. I did miss your mail though because you're the only one that writes back quick.

I was watching the news, and that's crazy how that fire spread out like that and burnt down all those houses. I didn't know that your parents and sister lived over there, I'm really glad to hear that they're okay. You're right there's going to be a lot more people homeless because 3,000 homes is a whole lot of houses burnt down.

I don't know when I'll be able to start working on my GED. I have to wait for them to assign me to a class, and it's a waiting list they go by until then I have to wait.

Thank you for the grammar tip. Just so you know sometimes I write like that because that's how I talk. But it's good to know because when I'm writing people like you or any of your friends I always want to write proper. When I write Luis or any of my friends, I write them ghetto because that's how we talk to each other.

I did get the Civil War book, Bible, and all the envelopes and paper you sent me. I have to say though you sent a whole lot of envelopes and paper. The CO got all butthurt when he gave it to me because it was a lot. At this prison anything that comes from Amazon they give it to you through a window like a package, it's not like the other prison where they give it to you like mail.

When he gave it to me he was like "What are you some kind of lawyer or something, next time order this shit through your package not through here." Then I said, "Why the fuck you getting mad at me, I didn't know." Then I just grabbed everything and left. But he can't get mad at things like that, that's his job. He's just lazy. Anyway, I did get everything though and excuse my language too. :)

Right now I don't need more questions. I still have some to write about. I'm going to be honest though I haven't been writing because I was writing about my relationship with my siblings. And I got stuck writing about Karla and Pedro so I stopped it I'm back on it now.

Thank you for the information on the restitution. I didn't see anything on there that can help me out but thanks anyway. But there's this new Senate Bill called SB620. It's on gun enhancements. Do you think you can send me info on that so I can send it to my auntie?

I got a friend in here and his mom got him a lawyer and that lawyer filed a petition called "For writ of habeas corpus." So if you have an enhancement that applies to that law you can basically get time taken off for the gun enhancement.

So I'm going to tell my auntie about it so she can help me. I don't have a lawyer at all right now, but I did have a paid lawyer. My auntie knows some lawyers, that's why I'm asking her for help.

I'm glad you got the letters. I'll just send you a couple every time I write you until you have them all.

Anyway, talk to you soon.

Take care,

Love,
Jorge

Oh and do you think you could send me two books of stamps please because I ran out. If you do just put them in the envelope with the letter when you write back. You can only send two books of stamps per envelope.

November 3, 2017

Dear Jorge,

Yes, I'm really glad that my family is OK. I'm trying to help others who lost everything. I think the final count is almost 5,000 homes burned down. It's hard to even imagine.

Before I forget, Mitali and I want to visit on Saturday, Dec 9th. Does that work? And what are visiting hours? Anything we need to know that's different than the other place? Are we OK on forms and everything?

So, I talked briefly to a criminal lawyer I met. I can't ask him much about your case because he's not your lawyer and I'm not paying him, but he had some advice on restitution. He said most restitution never gets paid so don't worry too much. He said it's fine for your auntie to talk to a lawyer but absolutely do not let your family pay a lawyer to try to negotiate restitution because they should save that money. He said they can't keep you in prison for not being able to pay, and they can't send you back to prison for not paying. And that it often doesn't get paid. So he said not to worry too much and don't pay anyone money to try to get it down. But if your auntie knows lawyers she can talk to for free, that's different.

I get the talking differently to different people. It's code-switching; you know that term, right? You can code-switch back and forth from English to Spanish and also from more formal to what you're calling "ghetto." It's a good skill to have because you can connect with all sorts of people. We all do it to some extent—like I talk differently to my friends than I do in a job interview—but it's more extreme for some people than others. So I can keep correcting grammar and stuff if you want (after all, I was your teacher!) or not, up to you. For example, when you're talking to Luis, saying "I don't have none" is totally fine. If you're talking to a lawyer or parole board or in a job interview, you'd want to say "I don't have any."

I actually think code-switching is super interesting because it seems like a sign of intelligence; someone's brain can work fast enough to assess a situation and determine for this context that this language will be more effective.

Here are some stamps; they're all I had but I'll send you more in the next letter. So sorry for causing problems from sending all the envelopes and paper! Amazon wouldn't let me send less than a certain amount, I guess because of shipping. I hope it didn't cause you any extra problems. And now you have paper and envelopes to share/trade with anyone else I guess. Or you can just write a *lot* of your life story.

I understand pausing on the writing. All of us do that sometimes when writing gets hard or emotional for some reason. You can always write about another subject—like choose some fun memories like some of our trips to the beach or the Exploratorium or something. Or you take a break and come back to it. I definitely don't want to pressure you. But at the same time, I really want everyone to read what you've written so I do want you to write fast! But really: do it at the speed you can.

I get why you were angry at the CO who was rude to you. But I do wonder (and obviously this is much easier said than done, no kidding) if it hurts you to be rude back? Is that something he can write you up for or anything? I think it's a natural way to react; I just don't want to see you get in more trouble. It sucks to have to be the better person, but is there any way to do it? Or do you just get too angry? This might be a terrible idea, but does writing about it help or no? That can also go in your life story.

I'll print something about "writ of habeus corpus" but I know nothing about it. What is your release date?

OK, I'll mail this and will send more stamps next time. Let me know how you're doing!

Love,
Bronwyn

November 12, 2017

Hi Bronwyn,

December 9th sounds good to me for you guys to come visit. The only thing different is that you have to make an appointment. They gave me your visiting approval so I'm going to send you your copy so you can know how it works.

Yeah, I'm not going to have my family pay a lawyer to negotiate restitution, I just wanted to know if there was a way to get it taken off. On the information you sent me last time for restitution it said that you can't really get restitution taken off, so I'm not worried about it no more.

Okay well I guess I'm pretty good at code switching, because I can change the way I talk really good with different people. Like for example the way I usually talk is way different from the way I talk to you on paper and in person. Or even sometimes you know when you're talking to someone that really isn't on your level, and you have to like "dumb down" to their level to have a proper conversation with them. That happens a lot in here. I don't have a proper way of saying it so I call it dumb down :) So I think I'm pretty good at code switching because like you said I can assess a situation and change the way I talk to fit in.

Thank you for the stamps and all the paper and envelopes. Don't worry, you don't have to say sorry because you didn't cause me any problems. I'm not going to share/trade with anyone, I'm just going to write a LOT like you said.

Sometimes I do take a long pause when I'm writing, but I'm going to try and do that when I get stuck, write about another subject. And don't worry, you're not pressuring me. Some people don't even get an opportunity like this so I'm going to try and focus on it as much as I can.

No, it doesn't hurt me to be rude back. And no he can't write me up for that because I didn't do nothing wrong. Don't worry, I'm not getting into any trouble. I do get too angry if somebody gets at me all crazy, then my first reaction is to get crazy back. If I don't, other people that were watching are going to think they can get at me like that and I'm not going to let that happen. That's why I just stick to myself. It's better that way.

I really didn't understand that information you sent me. I just want to know if my gun enhancement is going to apply to that new gun enhancement law. They're going to be taking time off your sentence for the enhancement if your gun enhancement applies to that law so that's all I want to know. My release date right now is January 9, 2030.

I don't know anything about making a book so whatever you think is good is good for me. That's fine, we can use "Jorge." Hopefully you take some Thanksgiving and Christmas pictures so you can send me some. So I can put them in my photo album.

So I'm sending you two of my letters back, some writing on my life story, and your copy of the visiting information. Talk to you soon.

Love,
Jorge

November 18, 2017

Hi Bronwyn,

I'm just sending you this quick letter because I wanted to ask you something. I was talking to my grandma and I was telling her that you are going to come visit next month on the 9th. The last time I saw my grandma was on July 2nd, a day before my birthday. When I told her you were coming she told me to ask you if she can come with you. I told her I don't know and I would ask you so can you call her and talk about it?

She hasn't been able to come see me because she can't find a ride and my uncle or auntie are always too busy. If my brother would go get his license, my grandma wouldn't have to be asking my uncle or auntie for a ride, they could just come up here by themselves. But it's not happening

Anyway, that's all I wanted to tell you. Talk to you soon.

Love,
Jorge

November 30, 2017

Dear Jorge,

OK, on Tuesday I'm going to call and see if we can make appointments to see you on December 9th, along with your grandma. If we can't get appointments that day, we'll try for December 23rd. It's confusing because it says that there's "open visitation" after 12:30 but I don't exactly know what that means. Does that mean anyone can visit then or only a certain amount of people? We obviously don't want to drive four hours if we can't definitely get in!

The part you wrote about Karla and Pedro was really powerful. Do you know what exactly happened to Karla? How is it for her to live with your grandma?

I wish I understood more about the criminal justice system to help you out, but I really don't.

I don't have many pictures from holidays so far but I have some amazing photos from autumn leaves and things if you want those! And of my dog. I don't seem to take enough photos of people.

Did I ever send you the *Chicken Soup for the Soul* book that I have a story in? I sent you the story printed out, I know. How are you doing on books? What have you been reading and do you need more?

This is going to be short because I'm not feeling very well and have a lot of work. Will write more soon but I wanted you to know that I'm in touch with your grandma and if it's not Dec 9th it should be Dec 23rd. And if you can explain this open visitation thing, let me know.

Love,
Bronwyn

December 6, 2017

Hey Bronwyn,

Yeah my grandma has been keeping me updated on the visit thing. Open visitation means that after 12:30 you can just walk in, that's what somebody told me but I'm going to double check and I'll let you know. My grandma told me you guys are coming this weekend so I can't wait to see you guys.

The only thing I know is that Karla's dad used to have her sleep with him in the same bed, then Pedro slept on the couch. That was the only thing that I was told. I don't think that nothing else happened but before something did happen my grandma took her away. I think Karla likes living with my grandma. She has her own room plus she gets anything she wants as long as she does good in school.

I don't mind the autumn leaves pictures and I also already have a few pictures of your dog. Why don't you like taking pictures? Almost everybody takes pictures nowadays.

No you haven't sent me that *Chicken Soup for the Soul* book yet. Right now I'm good on books. I'm almost done with the Nelson Mandela book, then I'm going to start reading the World War II book. Once I'm done with the Nelson Mandela book I'll let you know so you can send me another book.

Why aren't you feeling well, do you feel sick? Whatever it is I hope you feel better. :)

Anyway, thank you for the book of stamps you sent me. Can't wait to see you this weekend. Take care.

Love,
Jorge

December 15, 2017

Dear Jorge,

It was great to see you! Your grandma was so happy to see you too. I'm glad we could bring her and thank you for asking. She invited us both to your mom's anniversary rosary on the 28th and said if you want I can take pictures again and send to you. Let me know—might be the same as last year, but if you want the pictures, I'll do it.

You actually seemed pretty happy. I mean, I know you'd rather be out, but you seemed happier than I've seen you before inside. Do you think that's true? If so, why?

I found a website where I can put in a complaint to the department of corrections about the delay for your GED class. I won't do it without your permission, but I think it might be useful if you want. They should have gotten you into that a long time ago unless there's anything you're not telling me about trying to sign up.

How's the writing going? Now that I know you're not doing much, I want to see lots of writing. :) OK, and reading too. Let me know when you're ready for a new book or two.

What is Christmas like inside? You probably told me last year but I don't really remember. Is there any celebration or does it mostly feel sad to be in prison at that time?

I took my niece and nephew to Fairyland on Sunday. Did you ever go there when you were a kid? It's not very exciting as an adult or even as a big kid, but they're two and four years old and had a great time. There are a few animals there and they loved them, as well as a few tiny rides and little storybook houses. They were pretty excited about everything but liked the puppet show the best.

So, with no job right now, if you were not writing to people and getting books in the mail, what would you do all day? I know you can exercise, but what else? Is there a library? TV?

Yeah, I just don't love taking pictures of myself. I never look right in them! I'm not that critical of other people's photos, but the pictures of me are harder for me to deal with because I am critical of myself.

I was kind of getting a cold before I saw you and then I felt better, and then I took my niece and nephew to Fairyland and held their hands the whole time because they're little, and they were sick. So now I have a worse cold. But I'll be fine. I can rest over the weekend.

I hope you're doing well!

Love,
Bronwyn

December 16, 2017

Hey Bronwyn,

I just want to say thank you for coming to visit me, it really means a lot to me. I also appreciate you being here for me in these hard times. Receiving letters and getting visits from you really makes me feel a lot better. I hope you have a Merry Christmas and a happy New Year. Take care.

Love you,
Jorge

December 25, 2017

Hi Bronwyn,

It was good to see you too. I was happy to see all of you. I know my grandma was really happy to see me also. I'm glad you guys were able to meet her. I would love to get some more pictures of my mom's anniversary rosary.

I really didn't feel any different from the last time I saw you, but I have a better celly than I had over there so I think that's probably why. Plus, I work out a lot, so I think that helps too. And you know when you work out and you start seeing a difference in your body, that makes me want to work out harder. So it's not that I'm happier. I just feel better about myself.

I don't mind you putting in a complaint but then again I don't want these COs to start messing with me because of that complaint, you know what I mean? Plus my annual is almost here again so my points are going to drop and I'm going to end up leaving this yard anyway so if I did get put in school right now, I wouldn't have enough time to get my GED so I'd rather wait for my annual. So probably don't do it.

To be honest, right after I saw you guys, like a week after, I started feeling down and sad. You know because of the holidays and just thinking about my mom. So I haven't done any writing or reading but I promise to start again after this month is over.

Christmas in here is like a regular old day and it is sad when you think about it, but then again I tell myself I can't wait to get out. I'm just glad I didn't get life in prison.

Yeah, I don't think I ever been to Fairyland as a kid or an adult. Your niece and nephew are still very young so I'm pretty sure they enjoyed it. Is that Fairyland in Oakland?

I never liked taking pictures either when I was out, but I think I like taking pictures now. Just because, you know, later in the future you can look back at them.

I don't know what I would do if I didn't have nobody to write to or read. The only think I can think of is work out or watch TV. I have a 15" flat screen RCA. If I didn't have you to write I would literally have no one to write.[6]

Hope you feel better, being sick sucks. Especially being sick in here is worse. But I hope you feel better soon.

I wanted to tell you also that whenever you can if you can send me another book of stamps. Somebody was selling a bottle of cologne for a book of stamps, and it smelled pretty good so I bought it. So I'm all out of stamps now.

Yeah, I sent Emily a picture that I wanted a few copies of but I haven't heard from her in a while. I sent her a Christmas card. She's probably been busy because of the holidays and all. Hope to hear from her soon.

Well, I hope you had a good Christmas. I also hope you have a happy new year. Hope to hear back from you soon. I'm also sending a few of the old letters back, OK?

Take care.

Love,
Jorge

---

[6] Updated News for the Day: Jorge had about five other people to write to! —Bronwyn

December 28, 2017

Dear Jorge,

This is just a quick note because I'm leaving for vacation tomorrow. I wanted to let you know that I was able to go to your mom's memorial ceremony again, and Mitali came with us! I got some pictures of your family and will print them when I get back and send them. I didn't see Luis though; don't know where he was. Can you send me his new number?

Everyone wants to come visit you. The trouble will be seeing who we can fit in Mitali's car! She can fit five, so her, me, your grandma, and then I think Luis, Karla, Clarissa, and your Tia Gloria all want to come. Who do you want us to bring around Easter? I'm thinking your grandma, Luis, and Karla but let me know if that's not right. And Luis would have to commit because we can't just switch people, so if he says he's going to go, he has to. (Has he found his ID yet?)

I was wondering if you can find out a couple things about visiting, if you can.

First, if we bring Karla, how do we make a reservation for her? I know for the rest of us, we had to tell them our driver's license or ID # over the phone, but she doesn't have one. I think for Karla we'd need a birth certificate, so can you make sure your grandma has one for her? If you know who to ask there about how to make the appointment on the phone when she doesn't have an ID number, let me know.

Then our other question is if Mitali visits your celly, can she say hi to you at all or only see him?

Those are our questions. The service/memorial for your mom was really beautiful. I hope you did OK on this anniversary. We prayed for you.

Love,
Ms. Harris

January 6, 2018

Hey Bronwyn,

Yes, my grandma told me that you went to my mom's thing with Mitali. Okay, I can't wait to get those pictures! Just so you know though, you can only send ten pictures per envelope. Luis went to visit my mom at the cemetery. He sent me a couple of pictures to my tablet.

Yeah, they've all been wanting to come, but you know Luis doesn't want to get his license so it's hard. OK, so two that I really want to see is Clarissa and my Tia Gloria. So I think it should be you and Mitali of course then my grandma, Tia Gloria, and Clarissa. For any kid that's a minor, a notary needs to be done by the parent saying they give authorization for my grandma to bring them.

To be honest, I don't think you need to give an ID# if it's a minor. I think you just need to let them know that you're bringing a kid. I'll make sure about that though.

I don't think I'll be able to say hi to Mitali, only wave at her from my table, but I think I'll be able to give her a quick hug if you guys stay until the visit is over.

Anyway, thank you for going to my mom's memorial thing. I did okay for her anniversary. I prayed too. Hope you had a good vacation. Talk to you soon.

Love,
Jorge

January 17, 2018

Dear Jorge,

I have been back from vacation for about ten days now and can't quite believe it! It was a great vacation. Like I said, I wasn't sure I'd like traveling alone or if I'd get lonely, but I loved it. I'm sure I'd get lonely if it was long enough but it was perfect. New Year's Eve was a little rough because everyone had friends and spouses and I felt very alone. But other than that, it was wonderful. Did I tell you I tried scuba diving?

Here are the pictures!

So Luis doesn't have any kind of ID right now? Not even the state ID that isn't a driver's license? He definitely can't come without that.

So, I forget if your celly is your age or older? Do you guys talk in Spanish or English? What do you talk about?

Can you explain to me how your annual works? Is that why you got moved last time? When is it, and when will you be moved if at all? I really hope you can start the GED classes sometime soon. I think you'll actually really like being back in a learning setting.

I got the letters you sent me that I wrote you. I can start putting them together and sending them back to you to look at if that works for you. I have talked to two lawyers about this, and they both say you totally have a right to publish anything while you're inside. They also both say they'd use a pseudonym if they were you just to be safe.

One says it shouldn't hurt chances of early release at all; the other isn't so sure. So it is something to think about. Obviously, if we use a pseudonym there's less of a chance of any problem but you never know what's going to happen. You're an adult and can make the decision between getting your story out and staying totally safe. I think you're being very fair in taking personal responsibility, etc., and that this will build a following for when you do publish your life story. But

I suppose there is the chance it could make things harder for you inside, and you are the only one who can make that decision.

Mitali also wants us to think about making your story fiction based on a true story, so that's another option but we'd definitely need her help for that, and I don't know if she has the time. So let me know your thoughts.

The second lawyer I talked to would like to know two things about your case to see if she can help. I don't want to get your hopes up at all because I can't pay her myself, but just in case she can help she wants to know:

Is your sentence fixed or variable? That is, is it nineteen years or nineteen to something? (like nineteen to twenty-one, for example)

What was the actual charge, and did you plead guilty?

As for visiting, we may try for Saturday, April 7th. It's still a while off but maybe tell your grandma that we're aiming for that if you don't mind? I never know what name to use when I call your grandma. Should I say, "Hi, this is Ms. Harris," "Hi this is Jorge's teacher," or "Hi this is Bronwyn"?

I talked to Karla and Clarissa. I know they both really want to see you. Karla might be sad if Clarissa goes first because she's been writing to you. But I know it's a hard decision, and it's a decision that only you and your family can make. Or it might come down to who gets notarized permission first and if Luis gets his license. Is your tia approved to visit?

I'm so glad you didn't get life. You will still have a lot of life left when you get out. I know it feels like you'll be super old but you'll still have time to have a life and a family and so many of the things you want.

How's the reading and writing going?

So, I got back from vacation and found out that my landlord is selling the house I live in. I've lived here for fifteen years, so that's kind of a shock and a real bummer. There's a tiny tiny chance I can find an investor partner and buy it. I hardly have any money, so I'd need someone who does have money and wants to make an investment. I don't even really understand how it works, but I'm meeting with a real estate agent on Friday to see. It would be awesome but very unlikely. I'll be looking for other places to buy or rent. Both are just so expensive here!

I think Emily is pretty busy with work and kids, but let me know if you want me to find out if she's been getting your cards and letters! I always feel like I'd be so much more tired with kids, especially after working with them all day. I'm not sure how teachers who are parents do it, especially single parents.

OK, let me know how you're doing and if there's anything I didn't answer!

Love,
Bronwyn

January 25, 2018

Hey Bronwyn,

I don't think I remember you telling me you were going on vacation alone. I'm glad to hear you had a good time by yourself. Sometimes you just need that alone time, you know? No, you didn't tell me you tried scuba diving. How was it? Sounds like fun!

Yeah, I got the pictures and the book of stamps, thank you. The pictures you sent me of yourself, did you take those while you were on vacation?

I'm not sure but I think Luis just got his ID again. You know how he lost it. Well, he reordered it. I think he got it about a week ago. I'll find out whenever I talk to him again.

My celly is fifty-three years old and we mostly talk Spanish in the cell. We talk about a lot of different things. He gives me a lot of advice and he's one of the best cellys I've had so far.

Okay, so here you go to an annual once a year. The annual is just to see how everything is going. Like if you dropped points or gained points. As you know already, the only way you gain points is if you get write-ups. You can also ask to get transferred to another prison, whether it's a level four or whatever. It all depends on your points.

Right now I'm at sixty-four points and I haven't got any write-ups so my points will drop when I go to my annual. I think level three starts at fifty-nine points so I'll be level three for sure hopefully. That's all it right there. That's the only thing that goes on at your annual. Yes, that is why I got moved last time.

My annual is in June. I'm not sure exactly if I'll get moved but we'll see when I go in a few months.

I know, I hope they get me into a class soon too. I really want to get my GED. I've almost sent you all the letters already but I've been only sending you the ones I got from you when I was at the other prison. That sounds good to me, sending them to me so I can look at them. Yeah, I don't think that would affect my release date at all and we can use a pseudonym if you think that's better.

Honestly, I don't think publishing my life story will affect anything for me in here. I don't even tell people that I'm writing a book because I don't like people to know what I'm doing.

Isn't fiction like not real? I don't quite understand what Mitali is saying.

Okay so they gave me nineteen years flat. Just nineteen. I had a lot of other charges but the ones that stuck and that I got charged for were the attempted murder on a peace officer which I got nine years for and a gun enhancement use of a firearm. They gave me ten years for that.

So look, I know you're not paying that lawyer but there is something I want to do and I already talked to my grandma so she's willing to pay if it's not too expensive.

All right, so a new law came out which is SB 620. It's for gun enhancements. They're supposed to take time off if you have the gun enhancement that qualifies for it. And I have the gun enhancement that qualifies for it. The only reason I know is because I have a friend in here that has the same enhancement as I do and he has a lawyer on the streets filing the motion to get time taken off for the gun enhancement.

Now you know how every charge has a low, mid, and max of time that they can give you for that crime? Well, they gave me the max for that gun enhancement which is ten years. I think the low, mid, and max for that gun enhancement is wo, five, and ten or something like that. But I know ten years is the max. My friend told me they weren't supposed to give me the max because it was my first time ever getting in trouble.

Also another thing they gave me that gun enhancement for use of a firearm, but I never shot a gun in that crime, so that's one of the reasons why I think I should have even more action to get time taken off.

So you think you can tell your lawyer friend about that to see if she's familiar with that or knows nothing about it. If she's familiar with it then maybe you can ask her how much she charges. I told my grandma I was going to tell you to call her if your friend says she can help. So then they can talk about the price if she doesn't charge a lot.

April 7th sounds good to me. Next time I call my grandma, I'll let her know that date. I'm not sure but I say you should use "Jorge's teacher." I think Karla is most likely the one that's going to come because she's already with my grandma so it'll be easier for her to get the notarized permission. Yes my Tia Gloria is approved to visit.

I'm so glad I didn't get life in prison either because I could have got life but God was with me and still is.

The reading and writing is going good. Right now I'm finishing up something I've been writing about my sister Marina, the one that got taken away from my mom a long time ago.

Yeah, that sucks to come back from vacation and hear your landlord is selling the house after you been living there fifteen years. I hope everything goes well with the meeting on Friday, and hopefully you find someone willing to invest in the house. I'll be praying for you.

Don't worry, Emily finally wrote me back, so she's been getting all my letters.

So let me know what your lawyer friend says about what I told you. By the way, yes I did plead guilty to my charges. Anyway, hope to hear from you soon. Take care.

Love,
Jorge

February 2, 2018

Dear Jorge,

First of all, I talked to the lawyer. She said not to let your grandma pay anyone. She will do it for you, and she is very good (and usually very expensive). She has someone who wants to pay if it is a case with a low-income family. She is finishing up another trial and then will find out about that SB 620. She isn't sure if it is retroactive (meaning it passed after you were convicted, so she isn't sure if it reaches back in time). If you can wait a few months, your grandma won't have to pay and you'll get a better person than your grandma could afford. What do you think? Have your grandma save that money for when you're out!

Well, I can't buy my house, even with an investor. I'm looking at some small condos. It would put me into debt, but not bad debt, if that makes sense. It would be an investment. The problem is that there are so many extremely wealthy people that they can literally just write a check for something that I'd have to get a loan for. So for the sellers, they'd rather take that. So I'm both looking at rentals and thinking about buying a condo. It's so expensive here right now, and you know I don't want to move. All my family, students, friends, and church are here. So thank you for your prayers. Uncertainty is really hard for me.

Also, I know you know this, where you live or stay can have such an impact on your mood. And I work out of my home, so it's good to be a good environment. It's harder to find a place when you have a dog, but I am SUCH a dog person that I've got to!

Vacation alone was so great. I mean, I did get a little lonely but the relaxation and solitude was worth it. Interestingly, I don't think I could do it in a cold place because I get more depressed, but in a warm area it was just lovely.

I did take those pictures of myself on vacation, I think. I can't totally remember what I sent you now! You're welcome for the stamps.

So, we can come on April 7th, we think. We can fit three people besides me and Mitali. So obviously your grandma and then you and your grandma will have to decide between Karla, Gloria, and Luis. Obviously make sure whoever comes will really come because it would be a bummer to save a space for them and then have them not come. No one can take their place if we used their ID. But you have time to figure that out.

I'm really glad you have a good celly right now. How often do they change that around? Do you think he'll be your celly the whole time you're there?

Thanks for explaining the points system to me; that makes more sense now. Will you try to move to another prison if you can? Do they let you request or no?

OK, I like that you want to move on with the book, I just wanted you to know the potential downsides and make the decision on your own. You are an adult.

If we do this, I'll have to find a contract lawyer so that we can figure out how to get you your part of the money. I don't know how that would work while you're in. I'm assuming it would go to your grandma. Or you can trust me and I can give you your part when you're out, but I'd rather not do that in case something happened to me. Or if I got super greedy (not likely, but you never know :)) So I'll look into that. Can your grandma sign her name?

I'll start putting our letters together and mailing you a few pages each time. Do you happen to have a red or blue pen? You can mark them up (those colors would show easier if you do). Cross out anything that is too private, just remembering that you do want people to see what your life is like.

Then your life story would be different than the book of letters. Thoughts? I was thinking we could publish the first two years of letters, so about June or July of this year. Then we could always do more if people read it. The scary thing about writing is that you have NO IDEA if anyone will read it or not. But it's awfully validating to hold your own book, no matter if you ever make a dollar on it. I still haven't made any money on my other book because it cost me so much to write. And yet it was 100% worth it.

Fictionalization would be like if we wrote a book with a main character like you, based on your life, but not exactly. So it would protect you more but it would not be exactly your words. But I have never written fiction, so I'm probably not a good person to do it. I wonder if Mitali might like to write a novel one day about a young man in prison from what she's learned. Maybe you should ask her!

So, no matter where I move to, it'll be more money and I'll need to cut down on expenses. But I can always buy you books. Do you need any now? What have you been reading? I read a book called *Lilac Girls* about a bunch of women who all ended up in concentration camps for different reasons during World War II. My favorite way to learn history is by historical novels more than just reading history books. You've been reading some history books, right? How have you liked them?

I showed the lawyer exactly what you wrote so she has all the information. She just has to finish the other trial first.

I'm trying to spend more time with my nephew and nieces lately. They are two-and-a-half, almost five, and almost eight. They are hilarious most of the time. My nephew is going to kindergarten in the fall, and he's been licking doorknobs in public places. Which is obviously disgusting and he's been getting sick a lot. I told him that he can't lick doorknobs in kindergarten. He asked what would happen. I said the kindergarten teacher might call his preschool teacher and ask if there's still room in preschool because he wasn't ready for kindergarten. His eyes got really wide and he said, "But I *want* to go to kindergarten!" So I think he's done licking doorknobs!

Well, I've got to go. Moving means I will have to work more to earn money and also spend a lot of time looking for places. But here are some pages of our book, and I'm excited! Send them back when you get a chance—with markups—and I hope you're doing well.

Love,
Bronwyn

February 17, 2018

Hi Bronwyn,

Yeah, I'm not going to let my grandma pay anyone if it's not for sure. If she's willing to help me, I don't mind waiting a few months.

So I'm not too sure if it's retroactive either, but it can also be filed if there's like an error in the case. That's how my friend's lawyer filed the motion for him. Like, for example, they gave me the ten-year gun enhancement for use of a firearm. First off, I never shot a gun that day, second I was the driver so how am I gonna be driving and shooting at the same time? Does that make sense? Either way though, my grandma has all my paperwork, so whenever the lawyer needs it, she can look at those and make copies of it.

That sucks, sorry to hear that you couldn't buy your house. Hopefully you can find a nice condo somewhere close. I know it must be hard after so many years of living there you know, like you said, all your family, students, friends, and church are all there. So I hope you can settle somewhere nice. I'll keep praying for you.

Yeah, that's why I hope you find a place that you're comfortable at because I know you work from home. Plus it is definitely harder to find a place with a dog, but you'll find one. Since I've known you, you've always had a dog so you can't just get rid of it.

I bet vacation must have been great alone. Even though you might get lonely, but after you start relaxing and clearing your mind, you forget all about being lonely.

April 7th sounds good to me. I been talking to my grandma and we agreed on Karla and my Tia Gloria. I'll find out if my grandma talked to Gloria or if she's done the notary thing for Karla, I should have the answers to that by the time you write me back. Luis just started a new job so he won't be able to come because he works weekends.

It's always good to have a good celly or else you won't be able to be comfortable. Honestly, you can move around whenever you want. Most likely he will be my celly until I leave. I don't plan on moving in this prison. I will most likely move to another prison because I want to be closer to home, but I really hate transferring. It sucks.

They do let you request. They let you pick two different prisons you want to go to, but they don't tell you which one you're going to exactly. But you go to either one.

Don't joke that anything's going to happen to you, I need you to be there for when I get out. Plus if you ever needed my part of the money I wouldn't mind giving it to you because you been helping me a lot since we started talking again.

Okay, I didn't have any red or blue pens but one of my friends let me borrow his. So anything I don't want I'm going to mark in red.

Publishing the first two years of letters sounds good to me. Like you said, we can always do more if people read it, but how are we going to know if people read it or not? Yeah, I don't know if anyone will read my book but at least I can put my story out and be able to say I wrote a book so I think it's worth it also.

Oh, okay, now I understand the whole fictionalization thing, actually that wouldn't sound like a bad idea. Yeah, next time I get a letter from Mitali I'll ask about this.

I bet most likely you're going to have to pay more money for a place to live and that sucks. Right now I don't need any books. I'm barely going to start reading that World War II book. The Nelson Mandela book was pretty good, I liked it. The book you read sounds like a good one. I like reading history books because I get to learn about how messed up things used to be. Or you get to learn about how people like Cesar Chavez or Nelson Mandela struggled for their equal rights and things like that.

Okay sounds good to me, but look my friend told me some more information about that law. So he said that that law SB 620 is not retroactive but that the gun enhancement is retroactive just so you can tell the lawyer that. Either way though she'll find out all that information when she's reading about it, so I'll be waiting for her whenever she's done with that trial.

That's nice that you been trying to spend more time with your nephew and nieces. Two of them are kind of big already, but the two-and-a-half-year-old is still a baby.

Yeah, that's definitely not good for your nephew to be licking doorknobs, especially in public places. Apart from it being disgusting, he can get really really sick! That's funny though. I think you did a pretty good job scaring him. I hope he's done licking doorknobs.

Well, it was nice hearing from you. I hope everything works out with finding a new place. Yup, I'll be sending those pages of our book marked up with that letter. And yes, I'm doing well, talk to you soon.

Take care.

Love,
Jorge

March 1, 2018

Dear Jorge,

Yeah, I'm going to keep looking for a place to live! Hopefully it'll happen. I'll let you know for sure!

April 7th sounds good. I need someone (Karla?) to text me photos for your grandma's ID again and your Tia Gloria. Does Karla have a state ID yet? Probably not, so let me know if that thing gets notarized. And I think Mitali is visiting your celly?

Yeah, vacation alone was great. You'll get your chance! When you get out you'll still be younger than I am now so you'll have time to do the things you want. Sometimes when I start thinking too much it's not good for me to be alone. Does that ever happen to you? But in general I love it. Especially if it's warm outside to relax. Where would you like to travel when you get out?

Which prisons are you going to request? This is for the summer, right?

No, I'm not planning on anything happening to me before you get out! I'm just saying if it did, I'd still want you grandma to get any money that there was from the book. Like I said, I don't think it'll be much but it doesn't matter as much as getting your voice out there. And having a book with your words!!

When the lawyer is ready to talk about your case, I'm going to get a second opinion from her making sure you can publish. The other lawyer I talked to said that in California, inmates have a right to publish from inside, but I want to absolutely make sure. And yeah, I'm glad you're using a pseudonym. She said she'll be more available in May, so I'll talk to her then.

I'm sending you some more pages to review! I got the part of your life story. I am so sorry that you don't know what's happened to Marina. Do you have any idea why she was taken away from your mom? The other thing I noticed besides how sad it was and how you miss her is how much of an adult you had to be in the situation. You were just a kid too, but you were put into the position of helping make adult decisions and doing adult tasks. That's hard on a kid. How do you think it has affected you?

OK, this is a busy weekend, so I'll get this out in the mail. Always good to hear from you.

Love,
Bronwyn

March 13, 2018

Hey Bronwyn,

So I talked to my grandma the other day and there was a change in plans. My Tia Gloria won't be able to come visit me, but my other tia wants to come. I don't know if you met her yet. She's already approved to visit and tomorrow she's giving a copy of her ID to my grandma, is that okay? Also tomorrow which is Wednesday, my grandma doesn't work so she is going to go get that notarized for Karla.

I don't know where I have your number at, so do you think you can call my grandma so she can have your number so Karla can send you pictures of their IDs? And I'm not sure if Mitali is coming to visit my celly. I sent her a letter. Ask her though if you can, that way I'll know and I can let my celly know too.

You're right about that when I get out I'm still going to be very young so I'll still have time to do a lot of the things I want. I want to have a family.

Yeah, that happens to me sometimes too, when I'm by myself I start thinking a lot.

Other than going to Mexico, I just want to travel anywhere, really somewhere far. There are so many places I want to see.

Well, like I told you before also, I really don't care if I make any money off the book as long as my voice gets out there.

I don't think there would be a problem if I published a book but you can make sure anyway. Well, when Katie is available for me in May if she has any questions for me, I'll be ready for her.

I reviewed all those pages you sent me. Everything seems good to me. I don't remember why Marina got taken away, but if I'm not mistaken, I think my mom got arrested when she was with my sister. Oh, matter of fact, I remember now. Okay, so at the time Marina got taken away, my mom was living with some guy named Ricardo, which is Clarissa's dad. So one day my mom was at their apartment with Ricardo and my sister Marina. They started arguing loud and Ricardo ended up calling the police.

The police showed up and Ricardo started acting like the victim, telling the police this and so they arrested my mom because she wasn't calming down. So since my mom was being arrested, the police asked her if she had anybody she can call to pick up my sister. She called my uncle but he wasn't able to do it for her. My mom asked Ricardo if he could take my sister to my grandma's house. The cop was giving him a chance to take her over there but sadly Ricardo chose not to take her to my grandma so they took her to child protective custody, all because of him. That's exactly what happened.

I was put in some pretty messed up situations my whole childhood and it has affected me in a lot of ways. It's kind of hard to explain to be honest.

Okay, so can you make sure you call my grandma so Karla can send you those pictures?

Talk to you soon.

Love,
Jorge

March 23, 2018

Dear Jorge,

I talked to your grandma and it sounds like neither of your aunts can come so it's just her, Karla, me, and Mitali to visit your celly. Hopefully everything will go smoothly with the visit. They sure don't make it easy for your family and friends to get to you, which makes me really sad. People need visitors and contact with their loved ones, especially when they're incarcerated.

I got the pictures of your grandma's ID but the pictures of Karla's papers haven't come through yet. I'll call your grandma tomorrow and ask again. I'm not good at speaking Spanish on the phone because I get nervous but she's very patient with me!

I'm so sorry about Marina. That kind of sadness is hard to live with. I can see how it would be hard to explain how this kind of thing (and the other situations you were put in) affected you. Does it help to try to talk/write about it at all or no?

I don't know if that kind of stuff is something you're comfortable sharing. It would help people really understand what you've been through and your perspective, but it's totally your decision. The more honest you can be, the more people will understand and sympathize with you, but it can also be hard to let people see into your life like that.

I'm also thinking of the honesty that needs to come when describing your mom. Obviously your mom had her issues and the things she struggled with. But she was also so loving and funny and talented. I think the more you can present both parts, good and bad (and in between), the more real she is to people reading your story and the more they will really believe everything you have to say. But it can be hard to present all the sides of someone we love who is gone.

I have been super sick with a cold this week, but the good news is that I found somewhere to live! I'm going to wait to try and buy a home. The prices are just too high right now and it's ridiculous. So I'm going to try to save money and rent. The place I found to rent is nice. It's a one-bedroom apartment, and more expensive than I want, but everything is expensive right now. It has sunny windows and allows dogs and is close to a park, the beach, and a bunch of restaurants. It has really high ceilings too which makes it feel bigger. So the trick will be to how to pay the increased rent and save, but that's my goal!

Besides the book of letters with you, I'm also working on a new book about what people can do to help schools and students. When people read *Literally Unbelievable*, they keep asking what they can do to help schools like ours and students like you guys. I'm going to be interviewing a bunch of principals and teachers and former students.

So I'm asking you: What would have helped? What would have made a difference to you? It could be about teachers, principals, after-school programs, counseling, food programs, ESL classes for parents, absolutely anything. What do you wish people had done for you, your family, and your classmates?

I'll see you soon! Probably we'll come around noon again because it's such a long drive.

Love,
Bronwyn

April 12, 2018

Hi Bronwyn,

It was really nice to see you again. I had a good time with my grandma, but it was messed up that they didn't let my sister in. I was really hoping to see her. I hope all that paperwork for my sister gets sorted out soon so I can see her.

OK so it sounds like Jamestown is a little closer to Oakland than Pleasant Valley. I guess I'll make my decision by the end of next month because I go to my annual in June.

Yeah, everything that happened with Marina and the situation I was put in at the time was messed up, but we couldn't do nothing about it. Honestly I don't like talking or writing about it, but if I talk about it, I can't just talk to anybody about it, you know.

Well it's something I really don't like sharing, but I think it would be good to put everything about my mom in the book. I think you're right about that though. I really haven't put that much thought into that part. Writing about my mom is going to be the hardest part, not because I'm not going to be honest but because I want to write about her being the perfect mom without the bad parts, you know. But I know I need to put everything in.

Like you said though, the more I present both parts, the more real she'll be to people reading the book. It will be hard writing about my mom but I'll do it. I'm just going to write about her last.

So yeah, it was nice to hear you found somewhere to live. That's really the best thing you can do right now is wait to buy your own home since the prices are too high. That way it gives you enough time to save up enough money. The good thing though is that since you were saying you have a lot of nice spots around where you live, you don't have to go far for much. I'd love to live that close to all those restaurants and businesses.

That's nice that you're working on a new book. I think it would kind of make sense to write a book on how people can help schools and students like us.

OK, so those questions are kind of hard to answer, but right off the top though, I think more after-school programs, counseling, food programs, and ESL classes for parents would have helped a little. I would have to really like sit down and think to answer those questions.

Anyway, the bad news is remember I told you I was going to take some pictures, one by myself and the other with a friend. Well turns out I didn't have enough to buy the pictures. I did have enough but I guess they charged me for something that I don't know of and I was three dollars short so I guess no pictures. It sucks. :(

I hope, well I don't know when you guys are planning to come visit again but I hope it's in June so maybe I can take a picture out on the patio. I didn't even know you can do that here. At the other prison you couldn't do that so it's cool.

OK, so I checked out those pages you sent me and everything looks good to me. I'm sending those pages in a different envelope just so you know.

Talk to you soon.

Love,
Jorge

April 18, 2018

Dear Jorge,

This will be quick but I wanted to give you my new address before it's too late.

Also I'll try to call your grandma but in case I don't get ahold of her, I called the social worker and she's actually left the county agency. A person I talked to said she had someone call your grandma in Spanish and explain what she needed to do. If she forgot or didn't understand, she needs to go to the clerk recorder's office to pick up the original birth certificate (with a raised seal on it). Then the letter of guardianship (again, it should have a seal on it) needs to be picked up at the court at the juvenile justice center in San Leandro.

I hope that helps!!

More soon,

Love,
Bronwyn

May 4, 2018

Hi Bronwyn,

Well I don't know if I'm able to write you at your new address yet because I don't know if you moved already but I am writing to the new one, so I hope so.

By the way, I told my grandma what you told me and she said she did get that call. I think she also said you agreed to take her to the center in San Leandro sometime this month or something like that. I hope it all gets sorted out though soon, because my grandma is her guardian now so she shouldn't be struggling to take my sister places, you know. It's not right.

Anyway, I hope you're at your new place and that the move went smooth and that you had enough help. I wish I could have been there to help. When I get out, I'll always help you. Oh and the stamp you wrote me with looks pretty cool.

Talk to you soon. Take care.

Love,
Jorge

May 7, 2018

Dear Jorge,

Well, I love my new apartment, which is pretty exciting. It feels very much like home already. I've got all my art hung up on the walls and Ruby has settled in. She won't sleep on her dog bed but on the carpet, so I'm always having to vacuum up her fur. Sometimes she sleeps on the bed but she is big enough that she doesn't fit very well.

The location of where I live is kind of fun, too. It's kind of in the business district so I'm across the street from McDonald's, which I don't like, next door to the pizza shop, which I do like, and down the street from a bunch of other restaurants that are pretty good. I'm also just a couple blocks away from a little beach and almost next door to a park.

So even though it's a lot more expensive, it's a pretty good place I ended up in.

How are you doing? Is it warming up there? You go for your review next month right? Have you decided which prison is your first choice?

I'm trying to help your grandma figure out Karla's paperwork because you know how badly your sister wants to come see you. I talked to a lawyer friend who told me that if I get the case number for the case that made your grandma Karla's guardian then she'll look into where we need to go to get the papers. And I found another friend who wants to pay any court fees that your grandma has to pay to get the papers. Isn't that cool? I love when people want to help people they don't know.

Have you been reading or writing much?

OK, I'm finishing this letter later. I saw your grandma's paperwork and talked to my lawyer friend and this is the question we need to answer: I don't know how to say any of these things in Spanish so if you can ask your grandma next time you talk let me know. Is she Karla's foster parent or legal guardian? That will make a big difference in the paperwork. Legal guardian is better but the paperwork I saw says foster parent, so I'm just not sure.

I really wish I knew better how to help your grandma. I just have so little knowledge about this stuff and then don't even know how to say a lot of the things in Spanish. And then the system makes it so awful. I'm really feeling for all of you tonight.

I walked the dog down to the beach and sat and prayed (and cried, too, because it's so unfair) for your grandma and all of you. I mean, I just think about how much she's had to deal with and what you and Karla have had to deal with, and it's just too much. It's so unfair to all of you. I wish I knew how to help more.

Well, didn't mean to end this on a sad note but if you talk to your grandma please ask her that question and let her know I'm really trying to help, but I just don't know how this system works. But I'll keep trying.

Love,
Bronwyn

May 26, 2018

Hey Bronwyn,

I'm happy to hear you love your new apartment. Yeah, once you have all your things in the apartment it starts feeling more like home. So Ruby found somewhere more comfortable to sleep, huh? That's funny though that she's making you work more by vacuuming all the time.

By what you say it sounds like you're located in a good spot. I love McDonald's. I'd rather eat that than pizza but I like both of them. I wish I could eat some McDonald's right now though. At least you don't have to walk far to go to the beach or when you want to eat out. I bet Ruby loves being close to the beach and park.

I'm doing good, but lately I just been thinking a lot about everything like what I been through and just about my mom and really I just can't wait to get out of prison. It is starting to get hot over here and it's really not even summer yet so this really isn't nothing. It just gets hotter.

Yeah, I go to my annual next month. I haven't yet decided which one I want to go to. Honestly, I heard somebody that went to committee say that one prison was closed for intake and that another isn't taking nobody that isn't high-risk medical. So I'll see what happens when I go. If worst comes to worst I'll just go to E yard right here at this same place. It's a level three, and then I'll just leave next year.

I told my grandma what you told me and she told me that yeah you had already told her about it so hopefully everything goes good with that so I can see Karla again. Yeah, I think that's really nice that you know a lot of people that want to help us. That's why like I told you before I appreciate everything you do and also all those people that are willing to help us out.

Honestly, I haven't been writing because remember I told you I was trying to finish reading those *Harry Potter* books so I won't have extra books for when I transfer. I'm almost done with the fourth book though so I think I will be able to write some more before I leave here.

Sorry but I forgot to ask my grandma that question you wanted me to ask but we been getting locked down a lot lately so I haven't been using the phone much either. When I call her again I'll ask the question, then I'll tell her to tell Karla to text you the answer so that way you'll know immediately (that's if you haven't found out yet).

Don't worry, you already do a lot by helping my grandma and I understand things can be difficult when you don't know a lot about things like that. And trust me, I know it can be even harder when you don't know how to say a lot of things in Spanish. I don't even know how to translate a lot of English words into Spanish, and I'm Hispanic so I know how you feel.

Sorry to hear that you were crying. I wish I could have been there with you. I want to be there for my friends. Sometimes I get like that too. I mean, I don't cry because I'm in a place where I can't show emotions like that but I do get sad. I just think about everything my grandma is going through, everything I been through and just me being locked up and I get real sad.

Being locked up is not good at all if you're weak-minded this place will tear you down. I'm not weak. I've been through a lot as it is already so I'm not going to break, I just have to go through a lot more. I just can't wait to get out of this place. I learned my lesson. All we need to do is try and find a way to get some time taken off and I'll be all right.

Anyway so look, I know your lawyer friend is going to help me out whenever she's free. But this is what is going on. Remember, I told you my friend had a lawyer file that writ motion but he got denied because his lawyer didn't attach another paper that he was supposed to. Well something just passed where they can't deny you no more, right, so there's this guy in here that's been down a long time or whatever and he filed for that writ and he got granted. They gave him a court date and everything so they can resentence him with less time.

So my friend paid this dude to do that writ for him and we sent it out already to the courts so now he's just going to wait for a response. My friend copied everything the dude wrote on the writ and my friend is gonna type it up for me so I can send it to the courts and see what happens. I'm not going to pay or nothing, my friend is going to do it for me. The worst that can happen is them denying it. If they do grant it then they give me a court date so I can go get resentenced with something lower, so that's good right? I thought I'd let you know about that.

Anyway I'm going to ask my grandma about that and I'm going to have my sister text you the answer. Sorry I took so long to write back too. Talk to you soon.

Take care.

Love,
Jorge

June 11, 2018

Dear Jorge,

You've probably talked to your grandma already but the good news is that we've figured out all of Karla's paperwork and your grandma is the official legal guardian of Karla! We have all the paperwork to prove it! Your grandma is a really amazing person; she just doesn't give up! I am so impressed with her. She doesn't speak English and she never got to learn to read and write, and she gets so much done and just never ever gives up.

Yeah, I do like the new apartment, and Ruby likes it now too. It has carpet, so I think she likes sleeping on the soft floor. I just wish she could keep her fur on and not shed all over the house!

If I'm still at this house when you're out, I'll take you to the beach and McDonald's, for sure. Ruby does love being close to the beach and the park—she loves to sniff all the smells, especially the stinky low tide.

Let me know when the lawyer contacts you. I don't know how she will but she will. Be honest with her about everything and tell her about any issues you have. Things like not being able to get in the GED class to get your sentence shortened, not having a job in the prison, etc. you could ask her advice about transferring prisons too.

I can imagine that thinking about everything you've been through is a lot. You know what I'm going to say, right? Write it down! I think we're going to try to come on September 8th. I know that's a ways from now, but I'm having foot surgery on July 5th, so I don't know if I'll be able to get around for a while.

How are the *Harry Potter* books coming? And how is your writing?

Your grandma is so patient with me and my Spanish! I do OK when I speak all in the present tense, but when you add in the conditional and future and past tenses, it's hard. Especially the conditional tense, which is something like "I would buy that if I had the money." It's rough! Do you have trouble with that kind of thing or just specific words? How good are you at reading and writing in Spanish?

Oh, I can imagine that you don't have the ability to safely show emotion there. I hope you'll find someone professional to talk to when you get out because you'll have a lot of thinking and talking to do to work through everything and a good counselor can help a *lot*. It's not a sign of weakness, just of getting healthy.

You sound pretty discouraged. How are you doing this week?

OK, I have to pack to go to Hawaii! I'm going with my brother and sister-in-law, niece, and nephew, and parents. It'll be super fun but that's a *lot* of family time. And traveling with kids is not necessarily relaxing! I'll send you a postcard if you want!

Love,
Bronwyn

June 17, 2018

Hey Bronwyn,

This is going to be quick because I just want to let you know what happened at my annual. So I went to my annual this month on June 6th, and those two prisons I wanted to go to weren't available. My points dropped back down to level three, so I didn't want to go further than this. So I told them to send me to the E yard right here at this same prison.

It kind of sucks because I wanted to go closer to home so I'm stuck at this prison for another year. Hopefully next year those two prisons are available so I can be closer to home.

Also, I finished reading those *Harry Potter* books so I'm going to start writing again, I remember where I left off so I'll just start there. I'm not sure when I'll be going to E yard but I will let you know whenever I do go. That way you can send me the last three *Harry Potter* books when I'm over there.

Anyway, I just want to let you know what happened at my annual. Talk to you soon, take care!

Love,
Jorge

July 21, 2018

Hey Bronwyn,

Thank you for the birthday card. It's all right, late is better than never.

How was Hawaii? Who did you go out there with? Were you able to see where the volcano erupted at? What happened to your foot that you're getting foot surgery?

Everything is going good with me. I got moved to E-yard already. I've been over here since the 6th of July. It's alright over here. There's a lot more programs. I just hope I get put in school faster over here because it's been a year already and they still haven't assigned me. Anyway, I might move to another building next week, so if I do I'll write to you then so you can have my new cell number.

Have you heard anything from the lawyer yet? By the way, I promise to start writing as soon as I'm in a cell that I'm going to be permanent at. Anyway, I just wanted to let you know I got moved already so I hope you recover well from your surgery.

Take care, hope to hear from you soon.

Love,
Jorge

July 28, 2018

Dear Jorge,

Well, I'm finally able to walk around more after the foot surgery, which is great because I am SO tired of sitting at home and looking at the wall! It's been pretty boring, and I'm sure you will understand when I say that it's really easy to get depressed when you have nothing to do.

Speaking of having nothing to do, how's the new yard? Will they let you go to school? I'm so frustrated that they haven't so far—let me know if you want me to look into how to make complaints.

Hawaii was good! I went with my parents, brother, sister-in-law, and their two kids (ages five and three). My sister couldn't come and was sad about that, but we couldn't change the dates because my brother's kids were in a wedding which is why they went in the first place. It was a lot of family time but it was really fun, especially with the kids. We were on a different island than the erupting volcano.

For my foot: I had a bunion, which is a pretty common issue with feet where on the ball of your foot, like the end of the big toe where it connects to your foot at the bottom, the bone grows too much and you end up with extra bone they have to shave off to stop it hurting. So they had to cut into it, shave the bone, cut the bone, and reattach it with a screw. You can see why it hurt! I have to wear the big walking boot for six to eight weeks, which is annoying, but at least I only had to use crutches for a few days. I miss taking walks though and I REALLY miss hiking.

As far as the lawyer, I talked to her, and your case is more complicated than she thought. She said that is because of the gun and gang enhancements and the fact that the shooting happened in a residential area so they take it really seriously because people (especially kids) could have been hurt or killed. That plus leading the cops on a chase make it more complicated. She was actually really surprised you got as good of a plea deal as you did. At least the gang enhancement was taken off and maybe more. She said that she would have expected more like thirty-five years to life. I am so glad you didn't get that! But she's looking into it and says she's just waiting for your trial lawyer to get back to her and she'll write you a letter with all your options.

She's really good so I'd go with what she says if I were you, but if it ends up being something you don't like, do NOT give up hope. There's going to be a new governor in California in January and that always brings changes, and you keep with good behavior and trying to get education, OK? That can only help you.

What else… I sadly have very little to tell you because my life has been so boring lately. I have a couple of random pictures from Hawaii to send you! There's a terrible picture of a sea turtle but it was so close to me. It was awesome!

The picture you wanted me to copy—I took a picture of it and took it to Walgreens and they didn't crop it how I wanted. So I'm going to redo it, don't worry. But here's the original back!

How about you? Tell me all about the new place, and if you need books!

Love,
Bronwyn

August 8, 2018

Dear Jorge,

I talked to my editor today about our book of letters and she is excited! I'm sending you some more letters; hope I'm not repeating but I might be. I need to go through and make sure things are spelled right and put in the pseudonyms. Then she wants me to write an introduction about how we met, etc. And she'd like you to write an afterword if you're willing.

The afterword is what would come at the end and not be a letter. It would be like a short (can be very short) chapter about three things:

What you'd tell your younger self or young kids in your position when you were in middle and high school

What you'd tell other people in prison who want to make their lives better

What you want people outside to know.

We can work on this together if you want and she will edit it just like she edits all my stuff. She's good at keeping the meaning of what the writer puts as well as their voice, just cleaning it up a little. But if you want the book out soon, that's the first thing to do. Is that ok?

I think you can do a lot of good with this book AND I'm so excited for you to have a real book in your hand that you wrote. Well, that you wrote half of.

I also wanted to give you the information for the Prison Law Office. The lawyer says that they can help with things like how to get you into training and GED classes and answer questions about any rights you have to education, appeals, etc. They only take letters so you can do it. It doesn't have to be email or phone.

I'll write more soon but I wanted to see if you want to make this book really happen, soon. I'll handle the other stuff. You just keep reading these pages and write those three things as soon as you can.

I hope you're doing well. I think we're coming to visit you Sept 8! Hopefully I'll be walking well by then.

Love,
Bronwyn

September 4, 2018

Hi Bronwyn,

Sorry I haven't been writing you lately. I just been so distracted and still getting used to this new yard. I'm really glad to hear you're able to walk around more, and yes I do understand what you mean. It's real easy to get depressed when you have nothing to do. Oh yeah, so it sounds like you had a really good time in Hawaii then. If you went with your family, that was a whole lot of family time I bet.

Yeah, the lawyer sent me a letter too, telling me I'm better off leaving it how it is and I shouldn't try messing with my case at all. It sucks but it is what it is. I can't never let myself get too excited for things like that because it's never a for sure thing. I already had that in the back of my mind anyway. I haven't even wrote her back because honestly I don't have anything to say but "thank you for trying."

Anyway, the good thing is I got put in school already, I only been going for like a week though. I had to talk to the counselor to make sure it happened or else I wouldn't be in school right now.

I'm going to write about those three things you told me about so we can get that book done. So after I write about that, the book is going to be ready to get put together? Anyway, I haven't been writing though at all lately. My mind has been somewhere else, but I'm going to get back on it because I need to get it done. I also want to get my GED too now that I'm in school. I need to take advantage of it, even though a lot of it seems really hard because I haven't done any of it for a while now and it kind of gets me upset. I'm just glad nobody I know is in the class I'm in because that way, I can focus.

Anyway, *Letters from the Inside* sounds like a good name for the book. I can't wait to see you guys on Saturday. I just wanted to send you this quick letter to let you know I'm still here. So I'll get to writing those three things and I'll send those letters back too. So talk to you soon/see you soon.

Love,
Jorge

November 22, 2018

Hi Jorge!

I just wanted to say Happy Thanksgiving and to make sure you're doing OK since I haven't heard from you in a while. Let me know how you're doing and I hope your weekend is good!

Love,
Bronwyn

November 23, 2018

Hey Bronwyn,

Happy Thanksgiving to you too also. I'm doing good I was sick for a couple of days but I got over it already so I'm good now. They gave us this weekend from school for the holiday but we'll go back Monday. It started raining over too, how's the weather been over there? Anyway happy to hear from you. Hope you had a Happy Thanksgiving and that you ate a lot of turkey. :)

Love,
Jorge

November 27, 2018

Hi Jorge,

I'm glad you're feeling better. Sounds like you're working pretty hard in your GED class, yeah? Does that take up most of your time? What kinds of things are you studying? I'd love to hear more about it.

So, about this book! I'm getting pretty far. Are you up for writing that end part like we talked about? I sent you the questions and you do not have to do perfect writing! Do not worry at all!

I'll get working on the cover and the introduction. Questions? Anything you definitely want on the cover?

Hope you're doing well.
Bronwyn

December 2, 2018

Hey Bronwyn,

Sorry I haven't been writing you lately. I've just been busy with school and I've been enjoying the little time I have left with my celly. He goes home next year in March so we have just been kicking back having a good time. He's the best celly I've had since I been locked up and you really don't come across good people like that in here. So we just been enjoying the time we have left with each other.

Honestly, I haven't even written my last part to finish off the book because I've been so distracted. Then this month is December. It's going to be three years since my mom passed away and that's hard for me, you know? It's crazy how time flies by quick. So I just wanted to let you know if I can put it off until next month.

I did start working on one of the questions though. I did a small draft on my tablet. I just have to put it on paper and finish it off. I'm still thinking of what I'd like on the cover of the book. The only thing I can think about is maybe like a broken sand glass thing that's like a time, do you know which one I'm talking about? Anyway, though, do you have any ideas?

Anyway, I hope you've been well and that you've been enjoying the holidays. Talk to you soon. Take care.

Love,
Jorge

December 10, 2018

Hey Bronwyn,

Yes, actually school has been very exciting to be honest. We're working on all the basics like language, writing, reading, math, and science. I do all my work when I'm at school. We had to do a test like a few weeks ago and I asked the teacher which subject does she recommend I take. She told me math because my scores in everything else are pretty high. So if I do good on math I qualify for the Hi-Set which is the test you take to get your GED.

Honestly though I haven't even been writing much. I just been really enjoying the last couple of months I have left to kick it with my celly, he's one of the best cellys I've had so far and he goes home in March so I just been really distracted. Plus its already December so I'm just going to put it off until next month then I promise to really get back on it for real.

I'm not sure what I'd like on the cover of the book though. What are some of your ideas? It's actually harder than I thought.

Love,
Jorge

December 13, 2018

Hi Jorge,

I'm so glad school is exciting! It can feel really good to learn, can't it?

I'm proud of you for doing well, but I have to say I'm not surprised at all :) You know I've always known you're smart and if you worked hard you could do anything. You really showed that potential when you were in my class and it's just too bad you didn't have the kind of easier life some kids have, or a life that really sets you up for success. Like if you had a study room at home and a safe quiet place to do homework, I wonder if that would have changed things? Either way, I'm so glad you're getting to it. You're proving that someone can rise above their circumstances and succeed no matter what and that is POWERFUL.

What's your celly's name and what's great about him? Where's he from? I'm glad you have someone good. I think Mitali and I are going to try to go visit your old celly after we see you on the 29th. Hopefully the block won't be shut down again. Do you know why that happened?

I am almost done with the introduction. I'll send it to you when I'm done so you can decide if there's anything you don't want. It's basically recapping why I wrote the other book, how I got back in touch with you, and how I was nervous to visit you. Then how it was so good to see you and how I felt like at first I was still writing to a kid who was my student and now I feel more like we're peers.

I think you have the questions I sent you for the end, right? You can send those to me either on the tablet or paper, whatever's easier for you, and we'll clean them up and give you ideas if you're stuck. Sometimes I send things to my editor with sections like [blah blah blah what should I say here] and she gives me ideas.

I don't really know about the cover either. We can just have the designer do it if you want, or let me know if you have ideas.

The other fun thing you get to write after we're doing is your dedication. Think of who you'd like to dedicate the book to and it can be more than one person if you want.

In other questions, do you need any fun books to read? I'm sure you're busy with school but of course let me know.

I went to visit my friends in Mexico who run an orphanage for Thanksgiving and it was pretty awesome. They're in a pretty poor part of Mexico, and a dangerous one where a lot of the narcos are, but since I'm always with them I don't feel unsafe. They have about twenty kids living there right now, and most aren't actually orphans but their parents can't take care of them because of drugs, medical issues, abandonment, or whatever. I've been visiting for eighteen years now so one thing that is really amazing to see is the kids who have grown up and now help out there or have jobs nearby.

Then I came back and went on an awesome hike near Pt. Reyes at an elk preserve. We saw elk, coyotes, and lots of birds. Let me know if you want photos of either trip!

I hope you don't mind that this letter is so long!

Love,
Bronwyn

January 5, 2019

Hey Bronwyn,

Yeah, it is actually really good to be learning again. There's a lot of things that I've learned since I been locked up that's school related, that I probably could've learned when I was going to school on the streets if I would've paid attention more. It's crazy. Now though, since I been locked up, I really wish I would have finished school and maybe even went to college. You know I think that would of been a really cool experience. I would've got into sports too like football or basketball.

By the way I been playing a lot of basketball too, I haven't played no sports since I been locked up because I dislocated my knee a few times so I was scared to run. But since I been taking my fitness serious lately and working out my legs, now I feel like my legs are stronger. Anyway, I do feel like if I would've had a nice little study room and maybe lived in a peaceful area I might of for sure finished school. Now all I can do is get as much education as I can while I'm locked since its free. After I get my GED, I'm going to get into college too.

My celly's name is Jeff. He's from Oakland and he is really cool, like we bond really good in the cell and we're always together. No I don't know why D yard was locked down. That always happens though, honestly.

I don't want to make the message really long because or else it'll take really long for you to get it.

I think that's going to be the best part of the book too, the dedication. I know one person for sure that's going to be on that dedication. Anyway we do have a Christmas break so I'll try and write then, OK?

Love,
Jorge

January 10, 2019

Dear Jorge,

I'm so happy to hear about your GED classes! Do they go by semester or month or what? What are the classes like? Are they more independent study or direct teaching?

I've thought about teaching in juvenile hall before but never done anything about it. I'm not sure if I'd be afraid or if teaching where I did (you understand!) prepared me. I don't really like teaching adults though so teaching in prison would not be my ideal job. I like kids better!

So, something I've never asked you: if you had the chance for any career any at all, if you had had all the opportunities, what job or career would you want? Just curious. When I was little I wanted to be a librarian because I thought it meant I could read books all day! Sadly my mom told me I had to actually help people.

I get to take care of my little niece and nephew this weekend and am super excited. They're ages three and five and are going to come spend the night. We're going to go to the beach and the park and make brownies and eat pizza. I love them a lot and they're really fun kids, but also exhausting.

Happy New Year by the way! Any New Year's resolutions? Do you do that? I went to Monterey for a couple days. It was SO beautiful. Have you ever been? Let me know if you want any pictures of the ocean to have; I know you don't get to actually see it. I've been trying to spend a lot more time at the ocean, since it calms me down like nothing else. Do you have a list of places you want to go or things you want to do when you get out? Does thinking about it and seeing pictures make you sad or encouraged?

Love,
Bronwyn

March 11, 2019

Hey Bronwyn,

I'm sorry for the delay on the letters and email. But we were on lockdown and the tablets weren't letting us send emails out because we needed to connect the tablets to the kiosk and we couldn't do that because we were on lockdown. And I didn't have any stamps. We got off lockdown earlier like around one so I went out there and connected to the kiosk.

Also I wasn't writing because remember I had that good celly that I got along really well with? He went home like a few days ago so know I'm gonna focus and do all my reading and writing. I have a lot to catch up on, plus I been studying a lot for the test to get my GED too. So that's why I didn't write but now that he is gone I been on it.

I hope everything is well with you though. Other than that I've been okay.

Once again sorry for the delayed response. I hope you're doing well.

Love,
Jorge

March 16, 2019

Dear Jorge,

No problem! I understand wanting to spend time with your celly. It must be hard when you get a good person and then they leave.

I'm doing pretty well. I'm ready for the weather to warm up for sure! I'm still liking my new apartment. I guess it's been almost a year now, so it's not that new. I love living alone.

No problem at all, just write when you have a chance. I hope you're doing well!

Love,
Bronwyn

March 28, 2019

Hey Bronwyn,

Sorry for the delayed letter. I'm barely getting time to really focus on what I have to now that my old celly went home like I told you. Anyway, the GED classes are going really good. No, they don't go by semester, it's just one class. All they do is give us books for all the subjects and we just do them. If the teacher sees that you score high on a certain test then she signs you up for the GED test. That's why I've been studying because I want to score high on the test so I can just do the GED test already!

They give us milestones too for every time we improve in the tests, and I already got one. They gave me two weeks and those two weeks get taken off your sentence so I was happy when I got it because that was my first one ever. So that's two weeks less I have to be in here.

Yeah, I think teaching kids is way better than teaching adults, especially in prison. There's a lot of people just in there playing, being loud, so I bet—matter of fact I know—the teacher gets irritated because they're grown men acting childish. But if you're there to really do what you have to, you'll get it. I'm trying to get mine before this year is over.

Well, honestly I've never really asked myself that question about careers and I really don't know all the careers that there are. But I think I would have liked to be a businessman or something like that. When I get out though, I want to get a job like in construction, welding, electrician, or something like that as long as it pays well.

So you loved reading so much that you wanted to be a librarian? I probably would have gotten bored being in the library all day.

I have a lot of other things that I'm working on so I have to do a little bit of everything. Really my main focus right now is trying to get my GED because they give you a three-month milestone so they take that off your sentence. Also the YOP [Youthful Offender Program] is supposed to start pretty soon too so I'm looking forward to starting the program. They said that last year they weren't giving people milestones for all the groups they make you do because there wasn't a sponsor, but this year we have a sponsor so we're going to get all the milestones so I'm happy.

My two New Year's resolutions for this year are getting my GED and getting more lean which means losing the little extra weight I have so I can get more cut. Other than that though, really just focusing on anything and everything I can do to reduce my sentence and get all the education I can get.

I like seeing pictures of the ocean, so you can send me some if you like. I'm not too sure if I ever been to Monterey; I can't remember. Honestly, I haven't made a list of places I want to go, but I for sure have a lot of places in mind. Sometimes thinking about it does make me sad but then I tell myself I know when I get out I'll be able to go anywhere I want, you know?

Anyway, I'm getting all your questions answered so I can send all of it at once, OK? It was nice hearing from you. Hope to hear back from you soon. Take care.

Love,
Jorge

AFTERWORD BY JORGE

There's a lot of things I've learned since I've been incarcerated. Some of the main things I've learned are not to take things for granted. I've learned how to have a lot of patience, and just how to make smarter decisions.

I say I learned how to not take things for granted because when I was on the streets[7] I didn't care about a lot of things as much as I do now. I was selfish, making decisions that benefited me and were hurting my family. Then, one day I made the worst decision I could have ever made, and it got me nineteen years in prison. I hurt my family through that poor decision I made, and now my loved ones have to suffer and live some years without me there. I just thank God every day he's giving me a second chance to get out and do things the right way this time.

I also learned how to have patience. I say this because when I was out there, I had a very big anger problem. If I didn't get things when I wanted them or when anything got me mad, my anger would always get the best of me and I'd lash out. Being in prison, the first thing I learned was patience, because in here you're not going to get or do things when you want. Everything in here is set for a certain time, and even with things being timed it's still not for sure that it's going to happen at that time. You never know when there's going to be a lockdown, because anything can happen for whatever reason. So, having patience was one of the first things I had to learn in here and I'm grateful for that because I feel like by having patience, you'll be able to accomplish anything.

I used to always make choices that weren't wise and that I knew were wrong. Now I'm always striving to make decisions that are beneficial for me long-term. That's why I'm always involving myself in all the educational classes they offer here. These are the three most important things I've learned in prison so far.

---

[7] As earlier, Jorge uses "on the streets" to refer to life outside the prison.

A Message to Others in My Situation When I Was Younger

First, I want to tell people that are in the situation I was in that *you're not alone*. I know sometimes things get really hard and you might feel alone, like nobody cares about you, like you're forgotten. But it's not like that at all. All you need to do is find someone you can trust, like a family member, a friend, maybe even a schoolteacher you might feel comfortable with, just anybody you can confide in to talk and express everything you might be going through.

I know you're probably thinking, "No, I'm not going to talk to anybody about it," but trust me, it'll help. I used to hate talking about my problems. I felt it was easier to hold it in than to say anything. But I've learned that actually talking about your problems is really helpful. It feels like a bunch of weights lifted off your shoulders, because you're not holding anything in, so you start to feel less stressed out. It also clears your mind to where it helps you on making smarter decisions.

Another thing I would say is stay in school. When I was going to school, I hated it. But as I got older and came to prison I realized that it wasn't even school that I hated. What I hated was simply asking for help when I didn't know or understand something. In school my hardest subject was math, and when I didn't understand something I'd get mad because I didn't know, and I'd be too embarrassed to even ask for help. I felt like all the kids would make fun of me for not knowing. That was the biggest reason why I dropped out of school.

Now thinking back, I wish I would have stayed in school and finished so that I could have gone to college. Instead, I robbed myself of that opportunity. I think going to college would have been the best experience ever because it would have been something totally different for me.

The good thing is that I didn't completely miss out on going to college, because they offer us college courses in prison. So, I still get to do college. I just won't get the full experience like I would have if I had done it on the streets.

Now the last thing I want to say is love your parents, especially if you were raised by both your parents. A lot of kids don't get raised by their parents, some just grow up with one parent, and others grow up with neither of them.

Unfortunately, I was one of those kids that grew up without either parent, but I'm fortunate and very grateful I had a wonderful and strong grandmother who was willing to take my brother and I under her roof without any questions. My grandmother raised my brother and I since we were little kids and she always made sure we had everything we needed like a roof over our heads. We always had food and things for school. We always had clothes on our backs, just everything you can possibly think of, she always made sure we had it. I appreciate and love her so much for that. She's a strong, powerful woman and she means the world to me.

I hope you take the opportunity to show your loved ones as much love as you can when you can, because it's a beautiful feeling. Once you're in a situation like I am of being in prison, and you can't even give your loved ones a hug, can't talk to them when you want, or see them when you want, that's when it hits you. You realize maybe you should have been there for your loved ones or should have showed them more love. So that's why I say love your family and show them all the love you can every day that goes by, because I know what it feels like not to have done it as much as I wish I had.

My Hopes for the Future

As of right now, I have eight years left to serve, and this year in April will be six years that I've been locked up. One of my educational goals right now is to get my GED, because apart from that being very useful when I get out, you get a six-month milestone for completing it, so that's six months taken off my sentence. That's another focus I have: trying to receive all the milestones I can so I can go home to my family earlier.

Right now though, I'm currently in an electrical vocational class. It's pretty cool and I've learned a lot of different things since I have been there. So far I have finished the first book, and you get a six-week milestone for it. But unfortunately that's the only book I'll be able to finish because I'm going to be going to a level two facility soon, so I'm not going to be able to finish the vocational program. The good thing is that if I go to another prison that has the electrical vocational class, I can pick up where I left off.

Plans for when I first get out will be to stay out of trouble, and to find a good stable job, and just spend time with my family. I say stay out of trouble because when I first get out, I'll be on parole, so I'll have to be doing really good in order to get off parole early. I want to get off that as soon as possible. Once I get off of parole, I'll be able to fully focus on my life and live in peace.

One of the hopes I have for myself when I'm out is to get myself into doing some type of career. As of right now, though, I'm undecided as to what type of career I want to do, but some of the things I'm interested in are welding, electrical, or construction, things like that.

I have a hope for kids in the future, and that is for schools to give more counseling to students. I know there's kids that go through a lot and come from dysfunctional families, and most of the time, those kids hate talking about their problems because they feel as if nobody is going to care about anything they have to say. And to be honest, that's where it all starts.

When I was a kid, I had a lot going on at home and I'd go to school as if nothing was wrong. I wouldn't talk about how I felt. I just would hold everything in. In elementary school, I had a counselor who would randomly pull me out of class to talk to me and ask me how I was doing. At first I was reluctant because I felt like it would be a waste of time to talk about it. And then once I was kind of starting to open up just a bit, I stopped getting counseling. I don't know what happened there, but I felt angry about it and went back to holding things in. I felt like if I had kept getting counseling, it would have helped me.

It's a good thing I was one of those kids who was fortunate to have teachers that actually cared about me in elementary school, because if it wasn't for my third-grade teacher, I wouldn't be here talking about my life story. She told me my voice needed to be heard. So here I am.

I also have something to say to people who wind up incarcerated for bad decisions you've made because you didn't have that support in your family because it was dysfunctional. And that's this: don't lose hope because you're locked up. Just stay strong mentally and turn this negative situation into a positive one by working on yourself and bettering yourself as a person. Take all the groups and education classes they have to offer. I know it can be really easy to lose hope, but if you put your mind and all your focus into all the classes and groups, your time will fly by and when you get released, you'll have a lot to show for it. You'll have the credentials you need to get a decent job on the streets.

When I got locked up and sentenced to nineteen years, I felt as if my life was over. I didn't care about anything. During this time I lost my mother in a fire, so I was just hurt and going through a lot of pain. I was at the lowest point of my life. But after a few years of being incarcerated, I healed a bit from losing my mom and just told myself I was going to do everything and anything to come home and to better myself as a person. That's why I'm taking advantage of all the good things being offered to me right now.

Another thing I'm happy and grateful for is my beautiful fiancée Joanna! She walked back into my life in February 2019. We were never anything on the streets, but we went to elementary school together. We never really talked then. It was always just "hi" and "bye." We saw each other when we got older a few times because she used to hang with my little brother here and there. For some reason though, it felt like there was something that always drew me to her. She was always on my mind.

When I got locked up is when we finally took the step of actually communicating, writing letters back and forth. She even came to visit me in the county jail a couple of times. Shortly after that, we lost all lines of communication due to the fact that I lost my property when I got moved. It took us four long years to reconnect. Even though it took us some time, we're both glad we've come back into each other's lives. This time around, we took the time to actually get to know one another as a person, sharing our pain and expressing our feelings about how it felt to lose a loved one.

We also took the step of expressing how we felt for each other. And since then she became my girlfriend and now we're engaged and happily in love. She's been here for me in all ways and I'm thankful for all she does for me. Most importantly I'm grateful for her letting me be her partner in life. I'm looking forward to our marriage and family and life outside these walls.

ACKNOWLEDGMENTS

Bronwyn would like to sincerely thank:

- Jorge, who has become a good friend and someone I truly admire. His bravery in honestly telling his story is a gift.
- Jorge's family and fiancée who have supported him while he's incarcerated
- Mitali Perkins for driving to all prison visits and being a fighter for justice. Also for sparking the idea for this book.
- Rebecca Kohn for researching pertinent statistics that tell the story of injustice.
- Dorian Peters for consultation on how criminal justice works.
- Christine Osborne and Philip Dangler for careful copy editing.
- Julia Watson-Foster for helping me focus and encouraging me both when I wrote and when I didn't want to write.
- Jonathan Henke for patient teaching and stellar webmaster skills.
- The writers' group To Live and Write in Alameda for helping me believe I'm a real writer.
- For my family, who has opened their hearts and minds to this story.
- Every single friend, reader, and casual acquaintance who has mentioned how important it is to publish Jorge's story.

Jorge would like to extend his gratitude to:

- Bronwyn Harris and Mitali Perkins for the support that you give me and my family. Also for the belief you have in me and for all the visits.
- My fiancée Joanna for always being there for me in every way.
- Mr. Smith for all his help back in the day.
- Mrs. Willard, Ms. Gibbs, Mr. Guikema, and all other teachers who believed in me.
- My godfather and my grandma for raising me..
- For all my brothers and sisters: I know my life decisions made an impact in your lives. Please know that I love you all very much.

AFTERWORD

As Jorge writes, he made poor decisions when he joined a gang and drove for their gunmen as they fired on police cars. He was barely 18 years old. No one was hurt in the incident and, despite the fact that Jorge never discharged his weapon, his conviction carried the weight of both California's "gun enhancement" and "gang enhancement" laws. While there is no denying the violence in which he was involved, that one event does not inherently make Jorge a violent criminal.

According to Prison Policy Initiative, a leading non-profit, non-partisan advocacy group, "California has an incarceration rate of 581 per 100,000 people (including prisons, jails, immigration detention, and juvenile justice facilities), meaning that it locks up a higher percentage of its people than many wealthy democracies do."

You can support Prison Policy Initiative's reform efforts and learn more about who is incarcerated in California and why on their informative and chart-filled web site at **https://www.prisonpolicy.org/** and by following @PrisonPolicy on Twitter.

Jorge has legal representation, but his conviction cannot be overturned; nor can his sentence be reduced as it was within all guidelines and statutes at the time he pled guilty, in 2014.

If you would like send a message to Jorge, please visit **http://bronwynharrisauthor.com/** and Bronwyn can pass along your words.

Please See the Appendix in *Literally Unbelievable: Stories from an East Oakland Classroom* for more organizations that are disrupting the school-to-prison pipeline.

"If no one is dead we can't do anything." ↓

- God is a cycle-breaker: Exodus
  - slavery - debt - rest [Sundays]   Oakland Cops.
- Punitive vs. Rehabilitative
- School Status app.